Systematic Word Study

for Grades 4–6

**An Easy Weekly Routine for Teaching Hundreds of New Words
to Develop Strong Readers, Writers, & Spellers**

Cheryl M. Sigmon

SCHOLASTIC

New York • Toronto • London • Auckland • Sydney
Mexico City • New Delhi • Hong Kong • Buenos Aires

Dedication

This book is dedicated to fourth-, fifth-, and sixth-grade teachers,
who give the gift of word knowledge to students each and every day.

And to my granddaughter Meg Truluck,
who is presently a fifth grader, learning firsthand about the power of words
from her parents and teachers. May you put words to good use in your life!

Finally, to my husband,
who supports my efforts and enriches my life in so many ways.

✳

Acquisition Editor: Joanna Davis-Swing
Editor: Sarah Glasscock
Copy Editor: Jeannie Hutchins
Cover Designer: Jaime Lucero
Cover Photography: Media Bakery
Interior Designer: Sarah Morrow

ISBN: 978-0-545-24161-8
Copyright © 2011 Cheryl M. Sigmon
All rights reserved. Published by Scholastic Inc.
Printed in the U.S.A.

1   2   3   4   5   6   7   8   9   10   40   17   16   15   14   13   12   11

Contents

Introduction

One of the most persistent findings in reading research is the extent to which students' vocabulary knowledge relates strongly to their reading comprehension and overall academic success.

—Fran Lehr, Jean Osborn & Elfrieda H. Hiebert

With most basic print and language concepts under their belts, fourth-, fifth-, and sixth-grade students are ready to move into more sophisticated aspects of word study. The lessons in this book are designed to help you engage students with words not only by having them look at the semantic features of the words but also by gaining greater understanding of the nuances and relationships these words present. At fourth, fifth, and sixth grades, students have the capacity to appreciate the complex nature of words—their multiple meanings, their use in idioms, their meaningful word parts and derivations, and the multifaceted relationships among them. Powerful instruction in some necessary high-frequency words, content vocabulary, and general academic vocabulary are embedded in each weekly lesson. The lessons provide a systematic, daily instruction in words, even within a limited time frame, which will motivate and engage your learners. Each lesson is structured to make the best use of the precious little time you have in your classroom to teach all that you must teach. Most important, the lessons will positively impact your students' confidence in communicating effectively and ultimately will increase their level of literacy achievement.

Which Words Need to Be Taught and Why

Isabel Beck recommends a system in which words can be separated into tiers for a teacher's consideration for instruction. Her research categorizes words into one of three tiers.

- Tier One words are those frequently used that require little if any direct instruction. These words are typically in the spoken and written vocabulary of students, although they may pose difficulty in reading and writing, generally because of irregular patterns.

- Tier Two words are words used across the curriculum in many domains and are sometimes referred to as academic vocabulary. Research suggests that students need to add around 700 of these words per year to their vocabulary to keep up with grade-level materials.

- Tier Three words are those used infrequently and usually applied to a particular subject of study. Research suggests that at least 400 of these be acquired yearly.

The words selected for this book touch on each of these categories, but, more important, the lessons expose students to far more words than those in Beck's tiers. The lessons are a springboard for more word exploration and can exponentially expand students' word knowledge in general. There is considerable consensus among researchers that students need to add approximately 2,000 to 3,500 distinct words yearly to their reading vocabularies (Anderson & Nagy, 1992; Anglin, 1993; Beck & McKeown, 1991; White, Graves, & Slater, 1990), and these lessons help support this. With a typical school year of only 180 days, teaching 3,500 words explicitly becomes totally impossible. However, you can use the activities in this book to expose your students to many additional words, sometimes through the discussion of meaningful word parts that have broader application and sometimes through using words as hooks to get students interested in pursuing their own engaging words to use.

The Power of Words Frequently Used at These Grades

Certain words in the English language are, out of necessity, repeated frequently. In fact, three little words—I, and, the—account for 10 percent of all printed words! The top 25 words account for one-third of all print. And, amazingly, 107 of the top high-frequency words account for half of all printed text (Zeno, Ivens, Millard, & Duvvuri, 1995)! These 107 high-frequency words are included in the first book of this series, which is geared to grade one. Students usually master these words in first grade; however, if they don't, teachers will need to provide additional opportunities for students to master those words, which will aid their reading and writing fluency. Otherwise, the gap is likely to grow as students move from grade to grade. As the list of high-frequency words changes from grade to grade, it increasingly includes a number of words with irregular spellings that pose potential problems for struggling students. Students may not need direct instruction to learn the meanings of these words, but they may need more exposure, practice, and spelling hints to process them correctly and for those words to become automatic to them.

How do we make good use of our knowledge about high-frequency words? It stands to reason that the more words readers and writers know automatically, the more fluently they will read and write. Building automaticity, or quickness, with high-frequency words means that the reader/writer does not have to stop and consciously labor over decoding or encoding to accomplish these processes. Our goal, even with the simple high-frequency words, is not merely to have students memorize the words for a test on Friday, but rather to have students process these words to the extent that they know them automatically for the long term. This automaticity comes only through repetition and multisensory engagement with the words and their features. And you will see that the activities in these lessons do just that—engage each and every learner!

Beyond merely building desirable fluency in reading and writing, the greater benefit of automaticity might be that the cognitive focus of the reader or writer can then be directed toward more difficult aspects of the processes involved—reading comprehension or writing craft. With basic sight words under control, students' minds are free to figure out relationships in text, characters' motives, the best way to begin or end a piece of writing, or the voice they need to use to convey a certain message. Depth of understanding in reading and writing stems first from the small but mighty word!

In this book, high-frequency words still receive emphasis, although the words used in these lessons are appropriate for the upper grades and are less common than the high-frequency words taught in primary classrooms. The lessons start with a balance—half high-frequency words and half content/academic words. As lessons progress, they are weighted on the side of content and academic vocabulary. From the first lesson, students need to use critical-thinking skills for answering questions you pose about the words. A few of the words involved in the activities may even be a bit difficult for some of your students, but those segments of the lessons are brief. The activities will challenge more advanced students without diminishing the interest and motivation of students who are less prepared for the challenge.

So, the high-frequency word itself is not a critical part of these lessons. What is critical is having students process the word so that it becomes automatic and using the word as a starting point to delve into more complex word issues.

Including Content Vocabulary and General Academic Vocabulary

In addition to high-frequency words, the 35 lessons in this book include a number of critical content and general academic vocabulary words. These lessons do not include all the content and academic words your students need to know, but they are among words that represent major concepts in grades four, five, and six, and which are shared among disciplines in classroom instruction and discussion.

The juxtaposition of familiar high-frequency words and less familiar content and academic words will help make the latter less intimidating to students as they attempt to understand and practice the set of words in each lesson. All words are analyzed and explored in a number of different ways to be both interesting and thought provoking.

The content areas represented most often in this book are math, science, social studies, and language arts. The correct spellings of these words, many of which are big words that might be difficult for some of your students, are not as important at this level as the correct spelling of the high-frequency words. For example, having all students spell *interrupted* without fail is far less important than having them know the meaning of this word and relying upon their knowledge of its word parts, including understanding that *inter-* means "between," which can transfer to other words with the same prefix. In their lesson, they will also discover that *interrupted*, a vivid verb, can be a good substitute for the word *said* in dialogue that they write and that the word relates to the word *rupture*. Researchers have shown that a mere 14 prefixes and suffixes account for approximately 75 percent of all affixed words (White, Sowell, & Yanagihara, 1989)! Just think of the power of teaching students these tiny bits of information. You give them the keys to unlock the meanings of the majority of the more difficult words that they encounter in their studies.

Many of the academic words and some of the high-frequency words are additionally challenging to students because they have multiple meanings. In fact, approximately 70 percent of the most commonly used words that we draw upon in our everyday lives possess more than one meaning (Bromley, 2007). The most common meanings of words in these lessons are discussed explicitly.

General academic words are those that are shared among all educators in your school— *explain, produce, decided, language, region, developed, difference, discovered, describe,* among others. Upper-grade students need to know these words, understand their nuances, and be able to read and write them.

Theme-Related Words

In this third book of a three-book series, a number of lessons are thematically related. Some of the themes are based on meaningful suffixes that will help students as they encounter words with the same word endings, such as *-ology, -ism,* and *-phobia*.

Additionally, themes are included to interest students in word etymology. Some lessons contain a Word History section based on words that originated with people's names, foreign words that are commonly used in the English language, and words that grew from Roman and Greek mythology. English is a rich language that is a blend of centuries of experiences and relationships for students to explore.

Some of the lessons are based on themes that relate to "real world" literacy, such as words commonly found on job applications, words used to explore a range of emotions so students can better express themselves, and words that relate to systems of government that they need to understand.

A number of theme lessons investigate words used to describe, including size, appearance, time sequence, and even interesting adverbs. These may enrich students' written and oral language use by helping them find more precise and sophisticated language.

Transfer of word knowledge is one important goal of these themed lessons; however, encouraging students to develop an appreciation of their language is, perhaps, the most ambitious goal of this book.

Concepts Taught and Reinforced in These Lessons

Each lesson revolves around a five-day plan. This plan offers a vast number of opportunities for your students to understand the complexities of the word level of communication. Further, the lessons provide hands-on, explicit instruction in most, if not all, of the state standards I reviewed before compiling this book and creating the activities.

Additionally, knowing a word by sight and sound and knowing its dictionary definition are not the same as knowing how to use it correctly and understanding it in various contexts (Miller & Gildea, 1987). Also, words are learned when new words can be connected to our existing knowledge (Bromley, 2007). The activities in this book seek to engage students so that the words in the lessons become known words—words that will transfer into other situations. The following elements appear in each lesson.

Day 1: Meet the Words

In this opening activity you introduce the words for each week and offer direct, explicit information about them and how this information should be used. The final word in many lessons have a brief Word History feature. Lessons 1–19 contain 10 weekly words, and Lessons 20–35 feature 12 weekly words. In this activity, students will do the following:

- recognize each word for the week
- learn why the words are important to know—whether they are high-frequency or content words
- understand how their knowledge of the words can transfer into their reading and writing
- learn how the spelling patterns of some words help us read and write many other words
- learn how to use the features of the words to their advantage, such as grasping the meanings of word parts that help unlock meaning of other words
- understand the language of word study—syllables, consonants, vowels, plural/singular forms, tenses, suffixes, prefixes, origins
- learn the derivations and etymology of words that are both interesting and useful in word study

Day 2 Activities

Word Combo

In this activity, you challenge students to fill in the missing word in a sentence with a word that is a combination of word parts from the two to four words listed below each sentence. In this activity, students will do the following:

- identify chunks of words—prefixes, suffixes and bases
- learn many new words
- discuss word parts and their meanings
- develop greater awareness of how words work

Clustering

You ask questions about all or some of the words and have pairs or groups respond. In this activity, students will do the following:

- analyze degrees of word meaning
- explore differences and relationships among words
- demonstrate their understanding of the meanings and nuances of words by categorizing and arranging them

Picture That

Students process the words by drawing sketches to show their meanings. In this activity, students will do the following:

- make a personal connection with the word
- represent words artistically
- use their creative talents
- apply critical-thinking skills

Day 3: Word Builder

In this activity, each student manipulates letter strips at your direction. They build many words, working up to a single word that can be spelled with all the letters. In building the words, students will learn to do the following:

- manipulate letters and sounds to create words
- use patterns of language to help spell new words. (Many of the words in each lesson are multisyllabic words, but these activities are not sequenced strictly by spelling patterns because that would not allow for the exploration of as many words as are needed at upper grades. A section at the end of the Word Builder activity provides some necessary exposure to particularly valuable patterns as well as alternate spelling patterns that have the same sound.)

 Systematic Word Study for Grades 4–6 © 2011 by Cheryl M. Sigmon • Scholastic Teaching Resources

- apply certain rules for spelling
- practice the language of word study—prefixes, suffixes, affixes, consonants, vowels, and so on
- build one- and two-syllable words as well as many multisyllabic words with your guidance
- learn and discuss new vocabulary words

Day 4 Activities

Linkage

Students see how many words they can find in a long chain of letters. This linkage includes weekly words as well as many additional words. In this activity, students will do the following:

- identify the weekly words in a unique context
- be challenged by finding as many additional words as possible
- learn new words
- enjoy competition with other students

Word Action

In these activities, students get to display their creative talents as they apply their knowledge about the week's words. Word Action asks pairs or groups to write their own script for a skit or create a comic to show their understanding of a word. In these activities, students will do the following:

- apply their knowledge of the words
- use critical-thinking skills
- demonstrate their creative talents
- use writing skills for an authentic purpose

Stump the Class

In this activity, you issue a challenge for each student, pair, or small group to analyze the words for the week to determine relationships among them. Students use critical-thinking skills to find and categorize these relationships. There are no limits to the relationships they can explore—physical features, semantic features, content-related connections, or even more personal connections they might make. Students may even relate the words to popular culture—which can help them process the words at a deeper level! The real challenge here is for students to find unique categories that will stump their classmates as they share their word groupings. This activity requires students to operate at the top of Bloom's Taxonomy, where they will do the following:

- create, evaluate, and analyze words and their connections
- use critical-thinking skills

- categorize words based on connections
- articulate the connections to others

Day 5: Word Smart

The Word Smart challenge is the culmination of everything that students have learned about these words throughout the week. They will demonstrate an understanding of the following:

- physical and semantic features
- meaningful word parts—prefixes, bases, and suffixes
- hidden words that may help students remember spellings
- relationships and connections among words
- parts of speech
- word origins
- word meanings

Basically, students show that they understand the words, have processed the words in a new and different way, and can have fun with and be challenged by the words as well. You may use this activity to offer clarification for students who need it. Lessons become appropriately more difficult, but they always remain multilevel in order to meet the needs of all your students.

On each day, you will teach word knowledge that empowers students to widen their grasp and use of the words—far beyond the immediate lesson.

Word Chart

Week	Words	Content Words	Words From Word Combo
1	it's, questions, problem, complete, caption, index, reference, citation, bibliography, book* (newspapers)	high-frequency words, general academic words, language arts words	intercom, vacationing, preference, autobiography, combination
2	since, piece, usually, friends, heard, accuracy, acute, computation, obtuse, quiz* (computations)	high-frequency words, math words, general academic words	amputation, believable, indecision, excitement, disagreeable
3	become, across, however, happened, adaptation, camouflage, carnivore, herbivore, omnivore, enemy* (behavioral)	high-frequency words, science words	expression, adaptation, temperature, customary, pentagon
4	whole, remember, early, reached, listen, amendment, document, constitution, preamble, jury* (representative)	high-frequency words, social studies words	ambulance, carpenter, requirement, invisible, outstanding

 Systematic Word Study for Grades 4–6 © 2011 by Cheryl M. Sigmon • Scholastic Teaching Resources

Week	Words	Content Words	Words From Word Combo
5	cover, several, himself, morning, vowel, fable, genre, metaphor, simile, mystery* (categories)	high-frequency words, language arts words	mystical, courteous, dedicate, translation, exceptional
6	true, hundred, against, pattern, numeral, composite, diameter, probability, quadrant, radius (tessellations)	high-frequency words, math words	duplicate, numerous, compensate, wilderness, assurance
7	slowly, voice, cried, notice, south, biome, biosphere, ecosystem, ecology, muscle* (environmental)	high-frequency words, language arts word, science words	endanger, intercept, mischievous, biologist, solitary
8	ground, I'll, figure, certain, travel, conjunction, judicial, legislative, executive, phony* (congressional)	high-frequency words, language arts word, social studies words	demonstrate, generosity, tradition, disaster, circular
9	English, finally, wait, correct, interjection, proofread, quotations, analogy, alliteration, nightmare* (alliteration)	high-frequency words, language arts words	decisive, graduation, destructive, precious, attention
10	quickly, shown, verb, inches, street, convex, exponent, parallelogram, vertex, nickname* (parallelogram)	high-frequency words, math words, language arts words	prediction, promotion, transformation, migration, endurance
11	decided, course, surface, produce, potential, kinetic, chemical, thermal, mechanical, crazy* (thermometers)	high-frequency words, science words	prominent, exportable, perishable, confidential, guardianship
12	yet, government, object, among, cannot, revenue, annex, boycott, immigrant, paragraph* (immigration)	high-frequency words, social studies words	contribute, instantly, inspiration, distracting, congratulations
13	machine, plane, system, brought, understand, hyperbole, idiom, superlative, clause, quarantine * (superlatives)	high-frequency words, language arts words	recently, confusion, captivity, maneuver, tragically
14	explain, though, language, thousands, equation, inequality, ratio, volume, equilateral, digits* (equilateral)	high-frequency words, math words, general academic words	photographic, organic, immunity, intestine, suspension
15	carefully, scientists, known, island, constellation, eclipse, cholesterol, carcinogen, translucent, husband* (cardiovascular)	high-frequency words, science words, health words	property, incubate, thermostat, tolerance, resistance
16	hostile, aggravated, belligerent, arrogant, callous, obnoxious, resentful, insensitive, spiteful, vindictive (disagreeable)	degrees of anger and hostility	
17	worthless, forlorn, lonesome, ostracized, alienated, dejected, depressed, estranged, humiliated, obsolete (depression)	degrees of sadness or negative feelings	
18	suddenly, direction, anything, divided, general, amiable, altruistic, charitable, empathetic, humane (charitable)	high-frequency words, emotion/quality words	

Week	Words	Content Words	Words From Word Combo
19	energy, subject, region, believe, exercise, ecstatic, enthusiastic, elated, gratified, vivacious (enthusiastic)	high-frequency words, feelings of joy, science words	
20	developed, difference, probably, written, length, dictatorship, monarchy, anarchy, aristocracy, autocracy, democracy, theocracy (dictatorship)	high-frequency words, social studies words, math words, systems of government	
21	reason, present, beautiful, edge, sign, asserted, cautioned, bellowed, interrupted, responded, taunted, demanded (complained)	high-frequency words, synonyms for *said*	
22	finished, discovered, beside, million, lie, perhaps, imperialism, fascism, communism, patriotism, capitalism, socialism (patriotism)	high-frequency words, *-ism* words	
23	weather, instruments, third, include, built, glossary, aquaphobia, hemophobia, claustrophobia, astraphobia, optophobia, amaxophobia (arachnophobia)	high-frequency words, words that describe phobias	
24	represent, whether, clothes, flower, teacher, couldn't, anthropology, cardiology, ethnology, dermatology, meteorology, psychology (cardiologist)	high-frequency words, words with the *-ology* suffix	
25	describe, although, belief, another, beneath, onomatopoeia, personification, herbicide, insecticide, bactericide, scissors, incision (personification)	high-frequency words, language arts words, *-cide* suffix and *cis* base words	exponent, discovery, dictator, conditions, determine
26	breathe, committee, desert, discussed, either, mesmerize, valentine, shrapnel, vandal, diesel, Braille, maverick (valentines)	high-frequency words, words that originated with people's names	indicate, excellent, prevention, majority, humongous,
27	embarrassed, enough, especially, everywhere, excellent, atlas, cereal, hygiene, mentor, panacea, volcano, electricity (embarrassment)	high-frequency words, words from Roman and Greek mythology	maverick, intellect, tactical, imagine, colossal
28	foreign, frighten, height, himself, humorous, cliché, ambience, bizarre, brochure, entourage, impromptu, debris (malapropos)	high-frequency words, French words commonly used in English	
29	hungry, immediately, its, knowledge, square, cafeteria, chocolate, hurricane, tornado, canyon, canoe, avocado (hurricanes)	high-frequency words, words of Spanish origin	plentiful, punishment, subdivision, motorway, reviewing

 Systematic Word Study for Grades 4–6 © 2011 by Cheryl M. Sigmon • Scholastic Teaching Resources

Week	Words	Content Words	Words From Word Combo
30	necessary, neighbor, ourselves, once, people, alcohol, magazine, colonel, incognito, alfresco, hamburger, schema (artichokes)	high-frequency words, words of Arabic, Italian, or German origin	ladybug, aggressive, antonyms, jubilant, beverage
31	receive, recommend, separate, themselves, usually, elegant, distinct, rugged, glamorous, grotesque, unsightly, shadowy (considerate)	high-frequency words, appearance words (adjectives)	stupendous, unsightly, distinctive, motionless, congenial
32	though, thought, through, throughout, you're, your, diminutive, colossal, enormous, microscopic, voluminous, immense (miniature)	high-frequency words, size words (adjectives)	alternate, escalate, overthrow, gigantic, magnetic
33	weight, where, seriously, quiet, oxymoron, applicant, employer, permanent, temporary, chronological, dependents, references (fringe benefits)	high-frequency words, figure of speech, words on employment applications	voluntary, withholding, incentive, internship, personnel
34	familiar, favorite, experience, tendency, ancient, continual, decade, intermittent, annual, periodic, sporadic, lengthy (afternoons)	high-frequency words, time words	identical, narrator, validate, inverted, mistrustful
35	because, divergent, Europe, ocean, adamantly, anxiously, brazenly, casually, cautiously, cowardly, cynically, eerily (insistently)	high-frequency words, interesting adverbs	continual, researcher, divergent, tolerate, rejection

* Word History words

Words in parentheses are the mystery words in the Day 3: Word Builder activity.

cover	fable
several	genre
himself	metaphor
morning	simile
vowel	mystery

a c e e g i o r s t

The How-To's of the Five-Day Weekly Activities

Here are the directions and materials needed for each activity included in your weekly offerings.

Day 1: Meet the Words

Materials: For each student: seal-top plastic bag and a copy of the word template for the lesson. Cut the word template as shown on this page and page 16 for distribution.

- Depending upon the sharpness of your scissors, you can cut 4–6 copies of the word template at the same time. Put copies of the template together. Then, along the horizontal dashed line, cut off the bottom strip of letters. Reserve the letter strip for the Day 3: Word Builder activity.

- Fold the copies of the template along the dashed vertical line so the words are visible.

- From the outside edge, cut toward the fold and stop within a half-inch of it. Do this for each of the words.

- Unfold the templates, keeping them together. From the bottom, cut along the dashed vertical line to within an inch of the top.

- The templates should resemble a rib cage and will stay intact as you pass them out to students.

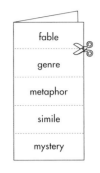

- Place a set of the week's words and letters in a plastic bag for each student. You can use a permanent marker to write each student's name on a bag. The bags don't have to be labeled, since they contain the same set of words and letters, but doing so can help avoid squabbles later.

- At the end of the activity, have students return their word cards to the plastic bag.

Directions: Direct students to detach the words on the template by pulling them apart. Encourage them not to attempt to tear with perfection, as you want this accomplished quickly. Then have students spread the word cards across the top of their desks or tables with the words faceup so that each word is visible. This will give them generous workspace and will keep elbows from knocking words to the floor as students work.

You will be sharing information about features of the words—plurals, double consonants, silent letters, and so on—as well as definitions and the relationships among the words. An asterisk indicates that a word has a brief Word History feature.

As you guide students through the lessons, you can easily offer appropriate support to differentiate the activity in a number of ways, such as the following:

- Ask students needing help to work alongside a partner who can support them. However, encourage all students to manipulate their own letter and word cards so that they stay engaged rather than becoming passive participants.

- Move close to students who need assistance so that you can guide them to think about the choices they are making.

- Give students permission to look at classmates' choices if they need help.

Day 2 Activities

Word Combo

Materials: the five Word Combo sentences in each lesson

Directions: Write the five Word Combo sentences and word choices on the board. Students find a word chunk from each of the word choices to combine into one new word that completes the sentence.

The bread is _ _ _ _ _ _ _ _ _ _. (10)
comfort<u>able</u> / <u>per</u>formance / standoff<u>ish</u>   (answer: *perishable*)

This activity is quite a challenge! Notice that the sentences don't offer a lot of context, which is necessary so that students don't guess what the word is. It's important for them to look at the word parts in each word choice and how to combine them. If you feel your students need more support, add more context to the sentences and/or model how you would complete the first sentence. Take time to talk about the new words and the many meaningful word parts that appear in this activity. As in the example above, the sound of a word part (in this case, *per*) may change subtly when combined in the new word. Point out this change to students. **Note**: The answers appear in the lesson, and the word parts are underlined for your information. Do *not* underline the word parts when you write the word choices on the board. Also, these words are not drawn from the week's words.

Clustering

Materials: lesson word cards

Directions: For this activity, you'll ask pairs or groups of students specific questions about the week's words. They will choose the appropriate word cards and arrange them accordingly. Then partners or groups will discuss their answers.

Picture That

Materials: targeted lesson word cards, paper and pencils

Directions: Tell students which word cards to use for the activity, for example, all the words ending in *-ism*. Then have them fold a piece of paper in half lengthwise and then into thirds to create 2 columns of 3 boxes. As you discuss these words and their definitions, students write a word in each box and draw a sketch that shows its meaning.

Day 3: Word Builder

Materials: letter strips detached from the word template on Day 1; you may either cut the letters apart and distribute them to students or have students tear apart the letters carefully.

Directions: Ask students to arrange their set of letters across their workspace. Call out each word in the sequence in which it appears and have students spell it. The words are sequenced so that they build upon letters and patterns. You may use all the words in the lesson or eliminate those that are too difficult or too easy for your students.

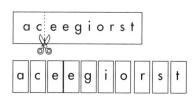

The last word you call out is the mystery word, which uses all the letters. Before students spell the mystery word, reveal the clue in the lesson to challenge them to figure out what the word is and to spell it without your saying the word first.

The second part of the activity usually focuses on spelling patterns in the words and other words that have the same pattern. As you have students spell the words, you may want to write the words correctly on the board and sort them by spelling patterns as you go.

Day 4 Activities

Linkage

Materials: copy of the week's linkage strip from Linkage Word Strips reproducible (page 127) for each student

Directions: Distribute the week's linkage strip and then have students glue it to a sheet of notebook paper. Tell them to find as many words as they can in the strip and write each word in a list below it. For most lessons, all the weekly words appear in the linkage strip; however, many additional words appear. Challenge students to see who can find the most words and to share the unique words they discover in the linkage. Allow about 10 minutes for this activity.

Word Action

Materials: writing materials for each pair or group

Directions: Direct pairs or groups to create a script for a skit based on one of the week's words. The challenge here is that the word must not be spoken. The rest of the class will try to guess the word featured in the skit.

Comics

Materials: a comic template for each student, pair, or group

Directions: This activity appears as an option in some Word Action activities. Create your own comic template or search the Internet for one and make copies for students. Have individual students, pairs, or groups draw their comic and use the highlighted words in the dialogue. Allow time for students to share and appreciate each other's work and discuss the different ways the words were incorporated.

Stump the Class

Materials: lesson word cards; a Word Clusters reproducible (page 128) for each pair or small group, one transparency (optional)

Directions: Students work together to find ways to sort the words into categories of their choice. The categories can focus on any characteristic—semantic, syntactical,

 Systematic Word Study for Grades 4–6 © 2011 by Cheryl M. Sigmon • Scholastic Teaching Resources

configuration, or any relationship they see among any of the week's words. Students don't have to use all the word cards, and they can use words more than one time. They should look at the words, search for a characteristic that some of the words share, copy those words into one of the circles on the Word Clusters reproducible, and then write the category underneath the words in the rectangle. Challenge students to find unique categories that will stump the rest of the class when the pairs or groups present their cluster of words. Once students have had time to create several word clusters, have each pair or group write their words—but not the category—in a circle on the board or on a transparency. The rest of the class should try to guess the category. Even though the guesses may identify a valid relationship among the words, the only correct answer for this activity is the one selected by the pair or group presenting it.

(**Note**: If you do this with an electronic whiteboard, you might write all the words in the box on the Word Clusters reproducible. Each time students share their words, they can use their fingers to drag the words into the circle, which takes far less time than having them write the words.

You can also assign this activity for homework. Have students write the words in the box on the Word Clusters reproducible. At home, they should group the words and fill in the categories. The next day, as time allows, students can challenge the class with their word clusters.

Day 5: Word Smart

Materials: lesson word cards

Directions: Ask students to spread the word cards across the top of their desks or tables with the words visible. This will also provide generous workspace for them and keep elbows from knocking word cards to the floor as they work. As you pose each question, students respond by searching for the answer among the word cards. They choose the word or words that answer the question and place them in their workspace for you to randomly check as you monitor the room.

Ask the questions and affirm responses at the pace you deem appropriate for your students. Praise their efforts liberally!

Maximizing the Impact of Your Lessons

Here are some hints that will help you make the most of these lessons:

- Be sure that *every* student participates in the lessons. Everyone should have the opportunity to manipulate the letters and words in response to your guidance. Remember that the lessons are multilevel to address individual needs of students across a range of achievement levels. If some students struggle with parts of a lesson, be sure to offer the support they might need to be successful.

- Remember that word exploration and vocabulary building are far more important than correct spelling! *Correct spelling is important only with the high-frequency words.* The goal is that students become familiar with the meaning-laden words in this book and can use them in different situations.

- Some students may need to rely upon others for help with what they don't understand. Facilitate this so that these students can learn as they go.

- Go beyond these lessons with your instruction and exploration. You still must teach vocabulary in your reading and content lessons; however, the analysis included in these systematic word study lessons should help your students notice additional features of the words and their meanings as well.

- Reinforce the words in these lessons at every opportunity. Repetition throughout the year is what will cause the words truly to be "known words" to your students. Here are some ideas for achieving that:

  o Point out those words during reading lessons.

  o Encourage their correct use in students' writings.

  o Post the high-frequency words on a word wall and the content words on cluster charts by subjects.

  o Make other teachers aware of the words that you consider critical for students' growth.

  o If you have spare time, review the week's words or review some of the words previously studied.

- Do all that you can to encourage incidental vocabulary learning! One of the most effective ways to accomplish this is to have students read as much as possible throughout the school day. The amount of time they spend reading is one of the best predictors of the size of their vocabulary (Herman, Anderson, Pearson, & Nagy, 1987; Miller & Gildea, 1987).

Above all, have fun with this systematic plan for developing the vocabulary and word knowledge of your students!

Bibliography

The American Heritage Dictionary of the English Language. (2006). Boston: Houghton Mifflin Harcourt.

Anderson, R. C., & Nagy, W. E. (1992). The vocabulary conundrum. *The American Educator, 16,* 14–18, 44–47.

Anglin, J. M. (1993). Vocabulary development: A morphological analysis. *Monographs of the Society for Research in Child Development, 58*(10), Serial #238.

Beck, I., McKeown, M. G., & Kucan, L. (2002). *Robust vocabulary instruction: Bringing words to life.* New York: Guilford Press.

Bromley, K. (2007). Nine things every teacher should know about words and vocabulary instruction. *Journal of Adolescent & Adult Literacy, 50*(7), pp. 528–537.

Flavell, L., & Flavell, R. (1995). *Dictionary of word origins.* London: Kyle Cathie Limited.

Herman, P. A., Anderson, R. C., Pearson, P. D., & Nagy, W. E. (1987). Incidental acquisition of word meaning from expositions with varied text features. *Reading Research Quarterly, 22*(3), 263–284.

Kipfer, B. A. (2007). *Word nerd.* Naperville, IL: Sourcebooks.

Lehr, F., Osborn, J., & Hiebert, E. (2004.) *A focus on vocabulary: Research-based practices in early reading.* Honolulu, HI: Pacific Resources for Education and Learning.

Miller, G. A., & Gildea, P. M. (1987). How children learn words. *Scientific American, 257*(3), 94–99.

Mountain, L. (2005, May). ROOTing out meaning: More morphemic analysis for primary pupils. *The Reading Teacher, 58*(8), 742–749.

Room, A. (1991). *The fascinating origins of everyday words.* Lincolnwood, IL: NTC Publishing Group.

Sarnoff, J., & Ruffins, R. (1981). *Words: A book about the origins of everyday words and phrases.* New York: Charles Scribner's Sons.

White, T. G., Graves, M. F., & Slater, W. H. (1990). Growth of reading vocabulary in diverse elementary schools: Decoding and word meaning. *Journal of Educational Psychology, 82*, 281–290.

White, T. G., Sowell, J., & Yanagihara, A. (1989). Teaching elementary students to use word part clues. *The Reading Teacher, 42*, 302–308.

Zeno, S. M., Ivens, S. H., Millard, R. T., & Duvvuri, R. (1995). The educator's word frequency guide. New York: Touchstone Applied Science Associates.

Recommended Web Sites

www.dictionary.com

www.rhymer.com

www.wordbyletter.com/suffixes_list.php

www.wordsmith.org

Day 1: Meet the Words

Have students pull apart the 10 word cards for this lesson and arrange them across the top of their desks. Then ask students to do the following:

- Hold up each card as you pronounce the word on it.
- Look at the word, read it aloud, and spell it with you.
- Return the word card to the top of their desk.

Provide a definition as necessary and share some of the word's features, as described below.

✳ **it's**: frequently used word; contraction for *it is*; not to be confused with *its*, which is the possessive form of the pronoun *it* ("It's raining outside." "The book is missing its cover."); identify apostrophe used in contractions

✳ **questions**: frequently used word and academic word; *q* is always followed by *u* in spelling (*queen, quest, quiz,* and so on); from Latin *quaestionem* meaning "a seeking, inquiry"; plural; 2 syllables; for discussion (*ask opinions*): "Questions are the foundation of all education." An interesting fact: *Q* is the only letter of the alphabet that does not appear in any U.S. states names

✳ **problem**: frequently used word and academic word; from the Greek word meaning "to throw before" and was considered a riddle that preceded academic discussion; 2 syllables

✳ **complete**: frequently used word and academic word; once spelled "compleat" and comes from the Latin word "to fill up"; prefix *com-* means "with or together"; adjective ("Your test is complete.") or verb ("Please complete this chart."); 2 syllables

✳ **caption**: academic word; a text feature: a title or brief description that appears under a graphic; *-tion* suffix indicates that the word is a noun; 2 syllables

✳ **index**: academic word; an organizational feature of text: alphabetic listing of people, places, and topics with their page number locations, usually found at the back of a book; plural is *indices*; 2 syllables; for discussion: "How is the index different from the table of contents in a book?"

✳ **reference**: academic word; adjective (*reference material*) which means "the source of information," or noun (*a job reference*) which means "someone who can testify to your ability or character"; 3 syllables; notice base *refer* and its connection to various uses of that word; suffix *-ence*

✳ **citation**: academic word; the source for a quote or information used, usually given in the bibliography of a text; multiple meanings: a legal document or a military honor; 3 syllables; *-tion* suffix indicates noun usage; base word *cite*

✳ **bibliography**: academic word; an organizational feature of text: lists citations for the origin of information, quotes, and ideas included in the text; *biblio* refers to the writing of books; *graph* means "written or drawn"; 5 syllables

✳ **book***: word history—*book* is the Old German word for beech tree (*boka*), which was used for writing letters. The word later referred to any writing. In the 1200s, when paper was used in England, any sheet of writing or collection of writing was known as a *boc*, and later called a book. (Sarnoff & Ruffins, p. 52)

Day 2: Word Combo

Challenge students to complete each sentence with a word that is a combination of word parts from each of the words listed below it. Each word must contain the number of letters shown beside the sentence. Discuss the meanings of some of the common word parts that students combined to make the new words.

1. Michael used the _ _ _ _ _ _ _ _ to tell everyone. (8)
   enter/invest/combination (answer: *intercom*)

2. We enjoyed _ _ _ _ _ _ _ _ _ _ _. (11)
   celebration/vacate/exciting (answer: *vacationing*)

3. Lea has a _ _ _ _ _ _ _ _ _ _ for strawberry ice cream. (10)
   refer/previewing/dependence (answer: *preference*)

4. It's too late for Lee to write her _ _ _ _ _ _ _ _ _ _ _ _ _. (13)
   biology/photography/automobile (answer: *autobiography*)

5. Do you know the _ _ _ _ _ _ _ _ _ _ _? (11)
   commerce/binary/international (answer: *combination*)

Day 3: Word Builder

Have students separate the letters at the bottom of this week's word template. Ask them to spell words as you call them out. Call out words in the order shown below. The final word should answer the following clue: These contain many text features every day. (*newspapers*)

nap

naps

snap

snapper

new

pew

spew

prawn

pan

span

spree

rap

wrap

swap

press

swan

swans

answer

answers

papers

newspapers

As students spell each word, write it on the board. Ask them to cross-check their spelling with yours and correct any errors. Then use the list to brainstorm more words that share the same spelling pattern, such as the following:

- *prawn:* dawn, sawn, withdrawn, yawn, lawn, pawn
- *rap:* snap, lap, stopgap, mishap, mousetrap, strap
- *press:* guess, excess, express, recess, distress, process

Day 4: Linkage

Tell students to see how many words they can find in the chain of letters on the Linkage Word Strips reproducible (page 127). The chain includes weekly words as well as other words. See who can find the most words and discuss the words that students think are interesting. You might ask students to write on the board the most unusual word they found.

Day 5: Word Smart

Ask students to arrange the week's words across the top of their desks with plenty of workspace below. Have them respond to your questions by picking up the correct word card(s) and holding it so you can see the answer. If there are more than two

correct answers, tell students to show only two—one in each hand. Ask: *Can you find . . .*

- a word that is a contraction?
- a word that is plural?
- a word hiding an unlawful act? (*problem*)
- a word with 5 syllables?
- a word hiding something a baby wears? (*bibliography*)
- a word with 1 syllable?
- a word hiding a journey to search for something? (*questions*)
- a word hiding something ball players wear? (*caption*)
- words that share the same suffix?
- a word with a prefix that means "together or with"?
- words that are features found in the back of a book?
- a word that has a word part that means "written or drawn"?
- a word that has the same suffix as *difference*?
- a word that names where you would find the page number for a topic in a book?
- a word that gives someone credit for their work?
- a word that names the place in a book where credit is given to work that is not the work of the author?
- a word hiding an antonym for *out*? (*index*)
- a word that started as a tree? (*book*)
- a word with 4 of the same vowel?
- a word hiding a way to show data in math? (*bibliography*)
- a word that names a brief description?
- words with suffixes that indicate they are nouns?

Now ask students to return the words to the top of their desks. Their next challenge is to sort the words by a common characteristic. Then have partners share their work by asking each other, "What's my rule?" The guesses may include valid categories, but the correct answer must match the partner's rule. Here are some sample categories for this week's words:

- *complete, caption, index, questions* (words with 2 syllables)
- *index, citation, bibliography, caption, reference* (text features/parts of a book)
- *questions, caption, citation* (words with the same suffix)
- *complete, reference, citation, bibliography, book* (words with 2 or more of the same vowel)

Day 1: Meet the Words

Have students pull apart the 10 word cards for this lesson and arrange them across the top of their desks. Then ask students to do the following:

- Hold up each card as you pronounce the word on it.
- Look at the word, read it aloud, and spell it with you.
- Return the word card to the top of their desk.

Provide a definition as necessary and share some of the word's features, as described below.

✳ *since*: frequently used word; tricky because same sound made by s and c; word often signals a cause-effect relationship in a sentence ("Since it's raining, we can't have our picnic."); also conveys a time element ("It has been two weeks since our history test.")

✳ *piece*: frequently used word; tricky because ie makes a long-e sound—in spelling this word, note that e is on both sides of the c; homophone for *peace*; synonym for *portion* or *part* (as noun); verb usage means "to mend or join," as in "Can you piece these paragraphs into a story?"; idiom usage: to give someone a piece of your mind

✳ *usually*: frequently used word; often slurred in pronunciation so that the 4 syllables collapse into 3—enunciate it clearly to aid in spelling; -ly suffix signals adverb usage; although the first syllable is pronounced like the word *use*, caution against inserting the e; adverb meaning "habitually," as in "We usually go to the movies on Saturdays."

✳ *friends*: frequently used word; plural form; tricky ie (To remember i before e with this word, keep in mind that fri<u>end</u>s are with us till the <u>end</u>.)

✳ *heard*: frequently used word; homophone for *herd* but difference is that <u>heard</u> relates to <u>hearing</u> and <u>ear</u>; past tense of *hear*

✳ *accuracy*: academic word used often in math; derivative of *accurate*; suffix -acy usually means "state or condition of," as in *piracy*, *legacy*; synonym for *correctness*; 4 syllables

✳ *acute*: word used often in math to mean "an angle that measures less than 90 degrees" (Each angle in an acute triangle is less than 90 degrees.) (*illustrate right and acute angles*); multiple meaning: can also mean "severe or sharp," as in "acute pain" or "acute appendicitis"; cu sounds like the letter name q; 2 syllables

✳ *computation*: word used often in math to mean "the act of computing or calculating numbers"; derivative of *compute* (verb); -ation changes verb *compute* into noun; prefix *com-* means "together or with"; 4 syllables

✳ *obtuse*: word used often in math meaning "an angle that is greater than 90 degrees but less than 180 degrees"; multiple meaning: can also mean "dull in intellect or in form"; 2 syllables

✳ *quiz**: word history—It is thought that this word originated from a bet made in 1780 by an Irishman who said that he could create a new word in the English language within 48 hours. He wrote 4 meaningless letters on the walls of Dublin, which created a frenzy of people asking about the meaning of this word. At first, *quiz* was coined to mean "a practical joke" and later took on the meaning of "trick or puzzle." In the U.S., it was defined as "a test." Remember that the letter q always has a partner in English words: *qu*. (Sarnoff & Ruffins, p. 52)

Day 2: Word Combo

Challenge students to complete each sentence with a word that is a combination of word parts from each of the words listed below it. Each word must contain the number of letters shown beside the sentence. Discuss the meanings of some of the common word parts that students combined to make the new words.

1. The tree doctor had to recommend an _ _ _ _ _ _ _ _ _ _. (10)
   comp<u>utation</u>/<u>amp</u>lify   (answer: *amputation*)

2. The story was _ _ _ _ _ _ _ _ _ _. (10)
   work<u>able</u>/<u>be</u>hind/rel<u>ieve</u>   (answer: *believable*)

3. Emma's _ _ _ _ _ _ _ _ _ _ was evident. (10)
   <u>in</u>side/in<u>cis</u>ion/<u>de</u>clare   (answer: *indecision*)

4. The crowd's _ _ _ _ _ _ _ _ _ _ grew. (10)
   <u>ex</u>it/govern<u>ment</u>/ in<u>cite</u>   (answer: *excitement*)

5. Do you know that _ _ _ _ _ _ _ _ _ _ _ _ person? (12)
   do<u>able</u>/<u>dis</u>tress/<u>agree</u>ment   (answer: *disagreeable*)

Day 3: Word Builder

Have students separate the letters at the bottom of this week's word template. Ask them to spell words as you call them out. Call out words in the order shown below. The final word should answer the following clue: You do many of these in math. (*computations*)

stomp

scam

out

scout
pout
spout
stout
amount
point
caption
action
campus
omit
coats
coast
potato
taco
point
panic
antic
custom
compost
tacit
catsup
atomic
mutation
computations

As students spell each word, write it on the board. Ask them to cross-check their spelling with yours and correct any errors. Then use the list to brainstorm more words that share the same spelling pattern, such as the following:

- *scam:* scram, exam, gram, sham, flimflam, swam, tram, wham
- *out:* shout, scout, pout, devout, without, blowout, flout, sprout
- *omit:* fit, bit, misfit, permit, submit, culprit, knit, cockpit

Day 4: Linkage

Tell students to see how many words they can find in the chain of letters on the Linkage Word Strips reproducible (page 127). The chain includes weekly words as well as other words. See who can find the most words and discuss the words that students think are interesting. You might ask students to write on the board the most unusual word they found.

Day 5: Word Smart

Ask students to arrange the week's words across the top of their desks with plenty of workspace below. Have them respond to

your questions by picking up the correct word card(s) and holding it so you can see the answer. If there are more than two correct answers, tell students to show only two—one in each hand. Ask: *Can you find . . .*

- a word that is an antonym for *enemies*?
- a word that is a homophone for a word that names a group of animals?
- words that name types of angles?
- a word that is a plural?
- a word hiding something thought to be immoral? (*since*)
- a word hiding the opposite of *begins*? (*friends*)
- a word that has 4 syllables?
- a word hiding a pronoun other than *I*? (*heard*)
- a word that means "sharp or severe"?
- a word with a suffix that indicates it is a noun?
- a word with the same word part as *oblong*?
- a word that may have originated because of a bet? (*quiz*)
- a word with a suffix that indicates it is an adverb?
- a word that names an angle greater than 90 degrees and less than 180 degrees?
- a word hiding a body part? (*heard*)
- a word that names an angle less than 90 degrees?
- a word that rhymes with *reduce*?
- a word where the letter *c* makes two different sounds?
- a word with a prefix that means "together or with"?
- a word that rhymes with *frizz*?

Now ask students to return the words to the top of their desks. Their next challenge is to sort the words by a common characteristic. Then have partners share their work by asking each other, "What's my rule?" The guesses may include valid categories, but the correct answer must match the partner's rule. Here are some sample categories for this week's words:

- *since, piece, friends, heard, quiz* (words with 1 syllable)
- *since, piece, obtuse, accuracy* (words with the same /s/ sound)
- *usually, accuracy, computation* (4 syllables)
- *obtuse, acute* (types of angles)
- *accuracy, acute, computation, obtuse* (math terms)
- *since, piece, usually, obtuse, quiz* (words that start with letters that come after *n* in the alphabet)
- *accuracy, acute, obtuse, usually* (words that start with vowels)

Day 1: Meet the Words

Have students pull apart the 10 word cards for this lesson and arrange them across the top of their desks. Then ask students to do the following:

- Hold up each card as you pronounce the word on it.
- Look at the word, read it aloud, and spell it with you.
- Return the word card to the top of their desk.

Provide a definition as necessary and share some of the word's features, as described below.

* **become**: frequently used word; compound word; 2 syllables; verb

* **across**: frequently used word; often used as a preposition ("across the river") though sometimes as an adverb or an adjective; spelling pattern helps with words like *boss, emboss, floss, loss*; 2 syllables

* **however**: frequently used word; often used to signal a relationship between two parts of a sentence such as, "We were considering taking the bus; however, the train was so much faster."; often used with comma (*demonstrate this*); compound word; synonym for *nevertheless*; 3 syllables

* **happened**: frequently used word; -ed suffix signals a past-tense verb; double consonant; 2 syllables

* **adaptation**: word used often in science; synonym for *adjustment*; in science, refers to a change in a species or an individual to better survive the environment, such as longer necked giraffes outlived other shorter necked giraffes (*discuss possible reasons*); -ation suffix changes the verb *adapt* into a noun; 4 syllables

* **camouflage**: word used often in science; means "disguising something that is normally visible," which is a way that many species survive (examples: Polar bears' white fur blends into their snowy environment. Some chameleon species change colors to match whatever they touch.) tricky spelling—remember *ou* vowel pair; 3 syllables

* **carnivore**: word used often in science; noun; means "meat eater"; mention this possible connection to *carnival*: In the 1500s, a Carnival was a celebration or merrymaking before Lent, when people stopped eating meat; word part *vore* comes from *vorar*, which means "to swallow or devour" in Latin; adjective form is *carnivorous*; 3 syllables

* **herbivore**: word used often in science; noun; means "plant eater" (*herb* will help students remember this); herbivores are primary consumers; adjective form is *herbivorous*; 3 syllables

* **omnivore**: word used often in science; means "eater of both plants and flesh"; adjective form is *omnivorous*; sometimes used in other contexts; prefix *omni-* means "all" as in *omnipresent* (Challenge: How does this relate to the point of view in literature that is called omniscient?) (Challenge: What does an omnivorous reader read?); 3 syllables

* **enemy***: word history—Dates back to late 1200s and came to English language from two Latin words—*in* or *en* meaning "not," and *amicus* meaning "friend." The word literally means "not a friend"! (Sarnoff & Ruffins, p. 17)

Day 2: Word Combo

Challenge students to complete each sentence with a word that is a combination of word parts from each of the words listed below it. Each word must contain the number of letters shown beside the sentence. Discuss the meanings of some of the common word parts that students combined to make the new words.

1. His _ _ _ _ _ _ _ _ _ _ gave it away. (10)
   creation/export/depressed   (answer: *expression*)

2. _ _ _ _ _ _ _ _ _ _ helped the butterfly. (10)
   aptitude/advertise/starvation   (answer: *adaptation*)

3. Please check the _ _ _ _ _ _ _ _ _ _ _ outside. (11)
   attack/pressure/temper   (answer: *temperature*)

4. Is this the _ _ _ _ _ _ _ _ charge? (9)
   custody/elementary/tomatoes   (answer: *customary*)

5. A _ _ _ _ _ _ _ names a shape and a well-known building. (8)
   onward/tagalong/pendant   (answer: *pentagon*)

Day 3: Word Builder

Have students separate the letters at the bottom of this week's word template. Ask them to spell words as you call them out. Call out words in the order shown below. The final word should answer the following clue: This is one type of adaptation. (*behavioral*)

oil

boil

broil

herb

herbal

rave

brave

bravo

blare

love

live

olive

alive

evil

labor

oval

rival

ravel

larva

larvae

viable

variable

behavior

behavioral

As students spell each word, write it on the board. Ask them to cross-check their spelling with yours and correct any errors. Then use the list to brainstorm more words that share the same spelling pattern, such as the following:

- *brave*: save, rave, stave, behave, concave, cave, pave, slave

- *blare*: care, nightmare, declare, cookware, square, aware

Day 4: Linkage

Tell students to see how many words they can find in the chain of letters on the Linkage Word Strips reproducible (page 127). The chain includes weekly words as well as other words. See who can find the most words and discuss the words that students think are interesting. You might ask students to write on the board the most unusual word they found.

Day 5: Word Smart

Ask students to arrange the week's words across the top of their desks with plenty of workspace below. Have them respond to your questions by picking up the correct word card(s) and holding it so you can see the answer. If there are

more than two correct answers, tell students to show only two—one in each hand. Ask: *Can you find . . .*

- a word with a word part that means "all"?

- a word with 4 syllables?

- a word hiding a vehicle? (*carnivore*)

- a word hiding a religious symbol? (*across*)

- a word hiding a word that signals a question? (*however*)

- a word hiding a plant such as thyme, rosemary, and basil? (*herbivore*)

- words that refer to what is eaten?

- a word that is in the past tense?

- a word that means "a plant-eating species"?

- a word that means "a meat-eating species"?

- a word that means "a species that eats plants and meat"?

- a word that is the antonym of *friend*?

- a word that can be a preposition?

- a word related to a celebration held before people temporarily stopped eating meat? (*carnivore*)

- a word used to signal a relationship in a text?

- a word that indicates that something will be changed?

- a word often followed by a comma?

- a word with a suffix that transforms it into a noun?

- a word that is compound?

Now ask students to return the words to the top of their desks. Their next challenge is to sort the words by a common characteristic. Then have partners share their work by asking each other, "What's my rule?" The guesses may include valid categories, but the correct answer must match the partner's rule. Here are some sample categories for this week's words:

- *carnivore, herbivore, omnivore* (share suffix that means "to devour or swallow")

- *adaptation, camouflage* (Camouflage is a type of adaptation, so both words deal with the survival of a species.)

- *across, happened* (words with double consonants)

- *become, camouflage, carnivore, herbivore, omnivore* (words ending in silent *e*)

Day 1: Meet the Words

Have students pull apart the 10 word cards for this lesson and arrange them across the top of their desks. Then ask students to do the following:

- Hold up each card as you pronounce the word on it.
- Look at the word, read it aloud, and spell it with you.
- Return the word card to the top of their desk.

Provide a definition as necessary and share some of the word's features, as described below.

* **whole**: frequently used word; tricky because /h/ represents its beginning sound; homophone of *hole*; generally used as an adjective

* **remember**: frequently used word; verb; synonym of *recall*; re- means "again"; 3 syllables

* **early**: frequently used word; both adjective ("These are the early results of the election.") and adverb ("We are starting the club early in the year.") usage; 2 syllables

* **reached**: frequently used word; verb, past tense of *reach*; multiple meanings; tricky vowel *ea* pair makes long-e sound; -ed makes /t/ sound; -each pattern helps spell words like *teach, preach, breach, leach, peach*

* **listen**: frequently used word; verb; tricky spelling because of silent *t*; 2 syllables

* **amendment**: word used often in social studies to mean "a change in a bill or a constitution"; in general usage, word refers to an alteration of a statement or document; -ment changes verb *amend* into a noun; 3 syllables

* **document**: word used often in social studies to mean "a legal or official paper" (noun): the Constitution of the United States is a famous document; also used as a verb with slight difference in pronunciation meaning "to support with evidence"; 3 syllables

* **constitution**: word used often in social studies; means "a documented system of principles by which a state, nation, or corporation operates"; word part *con* means "with or together" (Challenge: How does the meaning of *con* relate to *constitution*?); 4 syllables

* **preamble**: word used often in social studies that means "the introduction to a constitution"; in general usage, means "an introductory statement"; prefix *pre-* means "before" and word part *amble* means "to walk slowly"; *prologue* and *prelude* are also words that are used as introductions in books, musical works, and so on; 3 syllables

* **jury***: word history–This word refers to the 12 people who determine innocence or guilt in a trial. The word comes from the Latin word *juro* that means "I swear." In 14th-century England, each man who served on a jury had to answer a number of questions to show that he was eligible to serve. The answer to each question was "juro" or "I swear." (Sarnoff & Ruffins, p. 59)

Day 2: Word Combo

Challenge students to complete each sentence with a word that is a combination of word parts from each of the words listed below it. Each word must contain the number of letters shown beside the sentence. Discuss the meanings of some of the common word parts that students combined to make the new words.

1. The _ _ _ _ _ _ _ _ _ sped down the street. (9)
   bureau/amateur/finance   (answer: *ambulance*)

2. The _ _ _ _ _ _ _ _ _ finished the fence. (9)
   expensive/streetcar/enter   (answer: *carpenter*)

3. Is there a _ _ _ _ _ _ _ _ _ _ _ to join? (11)
   basement/reveal/inquire   (answer: *requirement*)

4. Jon felt _ _ _ _ _ _ _ _ _ in the crowd. (9)
   inference/credible/divisible   (answer: *invisible*)

5. The player was _ _ _ _ _ _ _ _ _ _ _. (11)
   standards/outfield/blossoming   (answer: *outstanding*)

Day 3: Word Builder

Have students separate the letters at the bottom of this week's word template. Ask them to spell words as you call them out. Call out words in the order shown below. The final word should answer the following clue: The United States constitution lays the foundation for this type of government. (*representative*)

interpret
interest
invest
prevent
patient
repeat
revert
train
strain
restraint
trainee

private

pirate

preteen

pretense

ripe

ripest

near

nearest

neat

neater

neatest

east

eastern

veteran

senate

representative

Review superlatives, using *near/nearest, neat/neater/neatest*. As students spell each word, write it on the board. Ask them to cross-check their spelling with yours and correct any errors. Then use the list to brainstorm more words that share the same spelling pattern, such as the following:

- *strain*: attain, disdain, abstain, terrain, unchain

- *pretense*: expense, nonsense, suspense, offense, defense

Day 4: Linkage

Tell students to see how many words they can find in the chain of letters on the Linkage Word Strips reproducible (page 127). The chain includes weekly words as well as other words. See who can find the most words and discuss the words that students think are interesting. You might ask students to write on the board the most unusual word they found.

Day 5: Word Smart

Ask students to arrange the week's words across the top of their desks with plenty of workspace below. Have them respond to your questions by picking up the correct word card(s) and holding it so you can see the answer. If there are more than two correct answers, tell students to show only two—one in each hand. Ask: *Can you find . . .*

- a word that is an antonym for *part*?

- a word hiding a group of people of one gender? (*amendment, document*)

- a word that is an antonym for *forget*?

- a word with a word part that means "to walk"?

- a word hiding its homophone? (*whole*)

- a word that is an antonym for *late*?

- a word with a silent *t*?

- a word with a prefix that means "before"?

- a word with a suffix that changes the base word, a verb, into a noun?

- a word that is in the past tense?

- a word that means "an introduction or statement that comes before the main message"?

- a word with 3 of the same vowel?

- a word with a long-*e* sound?

- a word with a silent beginning letter?

- a word hiding the name of a body part on either side of your head? (*early*)

- a word that often refers to a group of 12 people?

- a word that translates to mean "walking before"?

- a word that names documents or parts of documents?

- a word hiding the opposite of *begin*? (*amendment*)

- a word that is a synonym for *recall*?

- a word hiding the nickname of the person you call when you are sick? (*document*)

- a word that means "to pay attention"?

- a word that means "something added or changed"?

- a word that originated with the words, "I swear"?

- a word hiding a word that means "every one"? (*reached*)

- a word that is the fundamental principle that guides a state, country, or corporation?

Now ask students to return the words to the top of their desks. Their next challenge is to sort the words by a common characteristic. Then have partners share their work by asking each other, "What's my rule?" The guesses may include valid categories, but the correct answer must match the partner's rule. Here are some sample categories for this week's words:

- *remember, reached, amendment, preamble* (words with 2 or more *e*'s)

- *amendment, document, constitution* (words with *t* in the final syllable)

- *amendment, document, constitution, preamble* (words that relate to the organization of government)

- *constitution, jury* (words for things that ensure fairness in a democracy)

Day 1: Meet the Words

Have students pull apart the 10 word cards for this lesson and arrange them across the top of their desks. Then ask students to do the following:

- Hold up each card as you pronounce the word on it.
- Look at the word, read it aloud, and spell it with you.
- Return the word card to the top of their desk.

Provide a definition as necessary and share some of the word's features, as described below.

* **cover**: frequently used word; multiple meanings: "to extend over" ("She used a blanket to cover the child."), "to hide from" ("He tried to cover his tracks."), idiom usage: "blow your cover" ("The plain clothes policeman blew his cover when his badge fell out of his pocket."), "to provide protection" ("The soldiers' gunfire cover their comrade as he runs for the bunker."); adding a *t* to the end would change the word to *covert*, which relates to the second meaning above of *cover*—"secret, hidden, disguised"—as in "covert operations"; antonym is *discover* with *dis-* meaning "not"; 2 syllables

* **several**: frequently used word; adjective usually considered to mean "more than three but fewer than many"; 3 syllables

* **himself**: frequently used word; possessive pronoun; caution students against use of *hisself*, which is not a word; 2 syllables

* **morning**: frequently used word; originally (13th century) was the time before sunrise but now is the early part of the day before noon; noun ("Let's go to the mall in the morning.") and adjective ("Mother loves her morning coffee."); homophone for *mourning,* which means "grieving"; 2 syllables

* **vowel**: word used often in language arts; of the 26 letters of the alphabet, only 5 are always vowels (a, e, i, o, and u) and sometimes *w* and *y* are used as vowels; interesting note: Vowels are letter sounds made without any obstruction of air flowing from the lungs–try it!; every syllable has a vowel; 2 syllables

* **fable**: word used often in language arts; a short tale that teaches a moral with animals as characters; Aesop's fables are among the most famous; 2 syllables

* **genre**: word used often in language arts to refer to a category of text; pronounced ZHAHN-ruh; French word; examples of genres (plural): drama, mystery, humor, folklore, mythology, essays, speeches, and so on.; can also be used in other mediums, such as art; 2 syllables

* **metaphor**: word used often in language arts; a figure of speech in which two unlike objects are directly compared ("My car is a dinosaur." "She was his rock."); *meta-* means "after, behind" or "changed or altered"; 3 syllables

* **simile**: word used often in language arts; a figure of speech in which two unlike objects are compared using *like* or *as* ("His feet were as big as bales of hay." "Her tears flowed like a river."); word comes from the Latin word for *similar* or *like Note*: To help students remember the difference between simile and metaphor, tell them that a simile is the only one with an *s*, as in the word *as*, and an *l* as in the word *like*; 3 syllables

* **mystery***: word history–It originated from the Greek word *mysterion*, which came from an earlier word meaning "to have closed eyes and lips." It later came to mean "anything not clearly understood"; word used often in language arts; a genre characterized by a puzzling plot that remains unsolved until the end; in general usage means "something kept secret"; sometimes pronounced with 3 or 2 syllables (Sarnoff & Ruffins, p. 57)

Day 2: Word Combo

Challenge students to complete each sentence with a word that is a combination of word parts from each of the words listed below it. Each word must contain the number of letters shown beside the sentence. Discuss the meanings of some of the common word parts that students combined to make the new words.

1. The woman seemed _ _ _ _ _ _ _ _. (8)
   tiger/mystery/musical   (answer: *mystical*)

2. He is always _ _ _ _ _ _ _ _ _ to others. (9)
   courage/tedious/gorgeous   (answer: *courteous*)

3. We will _ _ _ _ _ _ _ _ the building to him. (8)
   vindictive/delicious/vibrate   (answer: *dedicate*)

4. I needed a _ _ _ _ _ _ _ _ _ _ _ of the letter. (11)
   laminate/transport/friction   (answer: *translation*)

5. The cupcake was _ _ _ _ _ _ _ _ _ _ _. (11)
   concept/complexion/excavate/disposal (answer: *exceptional*)

Day 3: Word Builder

Have students separate the letters at the bottom of this week's word template. Ask them to spell words as you call them out. Call out words in the order shown below. The final word should answer the following clue: Things that match fit into these. (*categories*)

age	greets	taco
rage	store	tacos
sage	storage	eager
cage	recite	agree
race	crease	erase
racist	create	secret
ego	crate	categories
egoist	cater	
greet	coast	

As students spell each word, write it on the board. Ask them to cross-check their spelling with yours and correct any errors. Then use the list to brainstorm more words that share the same spelling pattern, such as the following:

- *age*: engage, stage, rampage, storage

- *recite*: finite, dynamite, excite, cite, bite (*-ight* makes the same sound)

Also discuss words that have *-ist* added to the end of a base word and how it changes the base word to describe a person who has certain qualities or tendencies (*ego/egoist, race/racist*).

Day 4: Linkage

Tell students to see how many words they can find in the chain of letters on the Linkage Word Strips reproducible (page 127). The chain includes weekly words as well as other words. See who can find the most words and discuss the words that students think are interesting. You might ask students to write on the board the most unusual word they found.

Day 5: Word Smart

Ask students to arrange the week's words across the top of their desks with plenty of workspace below. Have them respond to your questions by picking up the correct word card(s) and holding it so you can see the answer. If there are more than two correct answers, tell students to show only two—one in each hand. Ask: *Can you find . . .*

- a word hiding a word that is the opposite of *under*? (*cover*)

- a word hiding a word that means "to cut off"? (*several*)

- a word that, if you removed one letter, would leave you with a happy face? (*simile*)

- a word hiding something you might do with your foot to a catchy tune? (*metaphor*)

- a word hiding a promise? (*vowel*)

- a word hiding a distance you might run? (*simile*)

- a word sometimes used as a greeting?

- a word that is a pronoun?

- a word that is a figure of speech comparing two unlike things using *like* or *as*?

- a word that is a figure of speech comparing two unlike things without *like* or *as*?

- a word that is an antonym for *expose*?

- a word that is a homophone for a word that means "grieving"?

- a word that names a genre?

- a word represented by one of the letters *a, e, i, o, u* and sometimes *y* and *w*?

- a word hiding a pronoun other than *I*? (*himself*)

- a word that if you added a *t* would mean "disguised or secretive"? (*covert*)

- a word that names a letter that is not a consonant?

- a word that names a short tale that teaches a lesson using animals as characters?

- a word that names a genre characterized by suspense and a puzzling plot?

- a word that is a compound?

- a word that names a period of time?

- a word that usually means "more than three but fewer than many"?

Ask students to isolate the word cards for *mystery, fable, metaphor, genre,* and *simile.* Then have them choose the word that best describes the following examples:

- Lincoln stood tall like a pine tree to deliver his speech. (*simile*)

- In this story, the grasshopper spends his time singing and playing while the little ant works hard to gather food for the winter. Winter finds the grasshopper dying of hunger, while the ant has a bounty of food. (*fable*)

- Our plan was a sinking ship! (*metaphor*)

- In this story, the steadfast tortoise wins a race against a lazy hare who plays and naps along the way. (*fable*)

- Biographies, essays, speeches, humor, fantasy, and realistic fiction are just a few examples of this. (*genre*)

- The private investigator gathered clues that finally helped her catch the burglar. (*mystery*)

- The old man's back was as gnarled and twisted as the trunk of an old tree. (*simile*)

Day 1: Meet the Words

Have students pull apart the 10 word cards for this lesson and arrange them across the top of their desks. Then ask students to do the following:

- Hold up each card as you pronounce the word on it.
- Look at the word, read it aloud, and spell it with you.
- Return the word card to the top of their desk.

Provide a definition as necessary and share some of the word's features, as described below.

* **true**: frequently used word; adjective usage; same sound as -ew, -ough, -eu; -ue helps spell words like *blue, accrue, construe*

* **hundred**: frequently used word; also used in math: word name for the cardinal number 100; 2 syllables

* **against**: frequently used word; preposition usage; 2 syllables

* **pattern**: frequently used word; also used in math; in general usage, means "a decorative design"; in math, it refers to a sequence of numbers or shapes; -ern has same sound as -urn and -earn; 2 syllables

* **numeral**: frequently used word; also used in math; means "a word, letter, symbol, or figure that expresses a number"; 3 syllables

* **composite**: word used often in math; means "a number that is a multiple of at least two numbers other than itself and 1"; *com*- means "together or with"; opposite of a prime number; prime and composite numbers are not to be confused with odd and even numbers ("The factors of 9 are 1, 3, and 9, so it is a composite."); in general usage, means "made up of parts," as in a composite sketch for a criminal suspect, which is made by putting together different types of facial parts to construct a whole face; 3 syllables

* **diameter**: word used often in math; means "a straight line that passes through the center point of a circle or sphere from side to side"; *dia* is Greek for "across" and *meter* is Greek for "measure"; (Challenge: What do the word parts mean in the word *diagonal*?) (*dia* means "across" and *gon* means "angle" = "across from angle to angle"); 4 syllables

* **probability**: word used often in math; means "the statistical likelihood of the occurrence of an event," as in "What is the probability that I will pick a blue cube from this bag of cubes of different colors?" or "What is the probability for rain today?"; probability is often represented by a fraction or a percentage; base word is *probable*; 5 syllables

* **quadrant**: word used often in math; means "one of four equal parts into which a plane (e.g., circle or square) has been divided"; *quad*- means "four" as in *quadrilateral, quadruplets*; 2 syllables

* **radius**: word used often in math; means "half of the diameter of a circle, or the distance from the center point of a circle to its outer edge"; comes from Latin word meaning "spoke of a wheel"; in general usage means an area of an operation such as "the radius of our campaign"; plural is *radii*; 3 syllables

Day 2: Word Combo

Challenge students to complete each sentence with a word that is a combination of word parts from each of the words listed below it. Each word must contain the number of letters beside the sentence. Discuss the meanings of some of the common word parts that students combined to make the new words.

1. We don't need to _ _ _ _ _ _ _ _ _ our efforts. (9)
   applicable/dutiful/mandate   (answer: *duplicate*)

2. The teacher gave us _ _ _ _ _ _ _ _ chances to fix it. (8)
   exercise/advantageous/numerical   (answer: *numerous*)

3. Getting a free dessert doesn't really _ _ _ _ _ _ _ _ _ _. (10)
   expense/composite/stagnate   (answer: *compensate*)

4. The vast _ _ _ _ _ _ _ _ _ _ presents many challenges. (10)
   trustworthiness/bewildered   (answer: *wilderness*)

5. Do I have your _ _ _ _ _ _ _ _ on that? (9)
   surely/aspire/substance   (answer: *assurance*)

Day 3: Word Builder

Have students separate the letters at the bottom of this week's word template. Ask them to spell words as you call them out. Call out words in the order shown below. The final word should answer the following clue: These are unique pattern designs. (*tessellations*)

taste

tasteless

late

lateness

latest

lean

leanest

neat

neatest

tonsils

saltiness

season

entitle

listen

stole

stolen

ease

tease

lesson

listen

aisle

siesta

essential

alien

satellites

tessellations

As students spell each word, write it on the board. Ask them to cross-check their spelling with yours and correct any errors. Then use the list to brainstorm more words that share a spelling pattern, such as the following:

- *neat*: heat, beat, meat, treat (*-eet*, and *-ete* make the same sound)

- *ease*: tease, please (*-ies* and *-eeze* make the same sound)

Review the changes in the words that have suffixes added (*taste/tasteless, late/lateness/latest, lean/leanest, neat/neatest, stole/stolen*).

Day 4: Linkage

Tell students to see how many words they can find in the chain of letters on the Linkage Word Strips reproducible (page 127). The chain includes weekly words as well as other words. See who can find the most words and discuss the words that students think are interesting. You might ask students to write on the board the most unusual word they found.

Day 5: Word Smart

Ask students to arrange the week's words across the top of their desks with plenty of workspace below. Have them respond to

your questions by picking up the correct word card(s) and holding it so you can see the answer. If there are more than two correct answers, tell students to show only two—one in each hand. Ask: *Can you find . . .*

- a word that rhymes with *blue*?

- a word hiding a word that names a place? (*composite*)

- the word with the most syllables?

- the shortest word in this lesson?

- the longest word in this lesson?

- a word hiding a synonym for "once more"? (*against*)

- a word with a word part that means "four"? (*quadrant*)

- a word that describes the number 9?

- a word that is represented by the spoke of a wheel?

- a word that is the opposite of *false*?

- a word that is demonstrated by at least three numerals?

- a word that is an antonym for *for*?

- a word with a word part that means "across"?

- a word that makes winning the lottery only a minuscule possibility?

- a word that means "parts that make a whole"?

- a word that fits in this sentence: "There is a _____ that the beagle will bark loudly."?

- a word whose plural has 2 *i*'s?

- a word that refers to a design?

- a word for the numeral that is greater than 99?

- a word represented by 1; 689; or 203,331?

Now ask students to return the words to the top of their desks. Their next challenge is to sort the words by a common characteristic. Then have partners share their work by asking each other, "What's my rule?" The guesses may include valid categories, but the correct answer must match the partner's rule. Here are some sample categories for this week's words:

- *composite, diameter, numeral, radius* (words hiding pronouns—*it, me, me, us*)

- *hundred, probability* (words with 2 of the same consonant)

- *numeral, composite* (words relating to numbers)

- *diameter, radius* (measurements)

Day 1: Meet the Words

Have students pull apart the 10 word cards for this lesson and arrange them across the top of their desks. Then ask students to do the following:

- Hold up each card as you pronounce the word on it.
- Look at the word, read it aloud, and spell it with you.
- Return the word card to the top of their desk.

Provide a definition as necessary and share some of the word's features, as described below.

* **slowly**: high-frequency word; -ly changes adjective *slow* into an adverb; 2 syllables

* **voice**: high-frequency word; usage: noun ("She has a lovely voice.") and verb ("I will voice my concerns to the principal."); -oice pattern helps spell words like *rejoice, invoice, choice*; used in language arts as a trait of writing that conveys a strong sense of the author's purpose

* **cried**: high-frequency word; past tense of *cry*: changes -y to -i and adds -ed

* **notice**: high-frequency word; usage: noun ("The notice was posted on the bulletin board.") and verb ("Did you notice her new sweater?"); 2 syllables

* **south**: high-frequency word; general usage as a direction; use capital letter when referring to the specific area of the United States

* **biome**: word used often in science; means "a large environmental community characterized by distinctive plants, animals, and climate conditions"; examples of biomes: tundra, ocean, rain forest, desert, savannah; word part *bio* means "life" (*biography, biology*); 2 syllables

* **biosphere**: word used often in science; means "the ecosystem of the earth—its crust, water, and atmosphere that support life"; word part *bio* means "life"; 3 syllables

* **ecosystem**: word used often in science; means "the system created by the interdependence of living organisms with their environment"; can be as small as a puddle or a tree or as large as an ocean; short for "ecological system"; word part *eco* comes from Greek *oikos* meaning "house or dwelling"; 4 syllables

* **ecology**: word used often in science; means "the study of interactions between living organisms and their environment"; word part *eco* means "house or dwelling," and -ology means "the study of" (*biology, paleontology, geology*); 4 syllables

* **muscle***: word history—The ancient Romans thought that flexing muscles looked like a little mouse running under the skin. The Latin word for "little mouse" was *musculus*, so that's how the word *muscle* came to be! Tricky spelling with the /sul/ sound spelled "cle"; 2 syllables (Sarnoff & Ruffins, p. 33)

Day 2: Word Combo

Challenge students to complete each sentence with a word that is a combination of word parts from each of the words listed below it. Each word must contain the number of letters shown beside the sentence. Discuss the meanings of some of the common word parts that students combined to make the new words.

1. That might _ _ _ _ _ _ _ _ our plans. (8)
   mana**ger**/**dan**delion/**en**able   (answer: *endanger*)

2. Will the football player be able to _ _ _ _ _ _ _ _ _ the pass? (9)
   ex**cept**/**in**clude/en**ter**tain   (answer: *intercept*)

3. The _ _ _ _ _ _ _ _ _ _ _ dog turned over the trashcan. (11)
   a**chiev**ement/danger**ous**/**mis**informed (answer: *mischievous*)

4. Mandy is studying to be a _ _ _ _ _ _ _ _ _. (9)
   logic/anti**bio**tic/perfection**ist**   (answer: *biologist*)

5. Staying in my room is like being in "_ _ _ _ _ _ _ _." (8)
   literature/**so**norous/elemen**tary**   (answer: *solitary*)

Day 3: Word Builder

Have students separate the letters at the bottom of this week's word template. Ask them to spell words as you call them out. Call out words in the order shown below. The final word should answer the following clue: This category describes many of this week's words. (*environmental*)

metal

mental

mantle

lineman

mineral

internal

interval

invent

remove

removal

lantern

antler

omen

meant

vote

voter

event

remnant

valentine

environment

environmental

As students spell each word, write it on the board. Ask them to cross-check their spelling with yours and correct any errors. Then use the list to brainstorm more words that share a spelling pattern, such as the following:

- *remnant*: constant, fragrant, gallant, infant, hydrant

- *valentine*: pine, fine, mine, incline, decline, outshine, enshrine

Discuss any new words and their meanings. Point out the different spelling of the same ending sounds in words such as *mental* and *mantle*.

Day 4: Linkage

Tell students to see how many words they can find in the chain of letters on the Linkage Word Strips reproducible (page 127). The chain includes weekly words as well as other words. See who can find the most words and discuss the words that students think are interesting. You might ask students to write on the board the most unusual word they found.

Day 5: Word Smart

Ask students to arrange the week's words across the top of their desks with plenty of workspace below. Have them respond to your questions by picking up the correct word card(s) and holding it so you can see their answer. If there are more than two correct answers, tell students to show only two—one in each hand. Ask: *Can you find . . .*

- a word hiding the opposite of *high*? (*slowly*)

- a word with 4 syllables?

- a word that names a direction?

- a word with a word part that means "life"?

- a word with a word part that means "the study of?"

- a word that shares a spelling pattern with *rejoice*?

- a word that comes from the Latin word for "little mouse"?

- a word hiding a shape? (*biosphere*)

- a word with a word part that means "house or dwelling"?

- a word that ends with a pronoun? (*biome*)

- a word that, if you changed the first letter, would mean "cooked in grease"?

- a word that, if you changed the first letter, would name a part of your face?

- a word hiding a word that means "an orderly plan"? (*ecosystem*)

- a word hiding something cold? (*voice, notice*)

- a word that means "the study of the relationship of living organisms and their environment"?

- a word that refers to something that could be found in the desert or forest?

- a word that is the ecosystem of Earth?

- a word that is in the past tense?

- a word with a suffix that signals that it is an adverb?

Now ask students to return the words to the top of their desks. Their next challenge is to sort the words by a common characteristic. Then have partners share their work by asking each other, "What's my rule?" The guesses may include valid categories, but the correct answer must match the partner's rule. Here are some sample categories for this week's words:

- *biome, biosphere* (same beginning part: *bio*)

- *ecosystem, ecology* (4 syllables)

- *biome, biosphere, muscle, notice, voice* (words that end in silent *e*)

- *voice, notice* (words that can be nouns or verbs)

- *biome, muscle, ecosystem* (words that contain an *m*)

Day 1: Meet the Words

Have students pull apart the 10 word cards for this lesson and arrange them across the top of their desks. Then ask students to do the following:

- Hold up each card as you pronounce the word on it.
- Look at the word, read it aloud, and spell it with you.
- Return the word card to the top of their desk.

Provide a definition as necessary and share some of the word's features, as described below.

✳ **ground**: high-frequency word; -ound pattern used in words like *mound, pound, sound*; usage: noun ("It was good to touch the ground after the long flight.") and verb ("His coach will ground him if he misses practice.").

✳ **I'll**: high-frequency word; contraction for *I will*, so it includes an apostrophe

✳ **figure**: high-frequency word; multiple meanings as noun ("George Washington was a great historical figure.") and a verb ("Let's figure out how much money we need."); 2 syllables

✳ **certain**: high-frequency word; used often as adjective; tricky spelling as -ain sounds like -in; based on Latin word *certus,* which means "sure or settled"; 2 syllables

✳ **travel**: high-frequency word; usage: verb ("Let's travel this summer."), adjective ("Set your travel alarm."), and noun ("Travel is our favorite pastime."); tricky -el ending sounds like -al or -le; 2 syllables

✳ **conjunction**: word used often in language arts; part of speech that serves to connect parts of sentences; review different types appropriate to your grade and curriculum: Coordinating conjunctions connect similar elements in a sentence—either words or subjects or verb phrases—and include *and, but, or, for, nor, yet,* and *so*. Correlative conjunctions also connect similar elements in sentences but are used in pairs such as *not only/but also, either/ or, neither/nor*. Subordinating conjunctions connect subordinate clauses to main clauses (" Our picnic has been canceled <u>because</u> of the rain."); 3 syllables

✳ **judicial**: word used often in social studies: one of the main branches of government made up of the court system responsible for interpreting the law; highest U.S. federal court is the Supreme Court, with 9 justices; adjective; relates to *justice* and *judgment*; 3 syllables

✳ **legislative**: word used often in social studies: one of the main branches of government made up of Congress, which comprises the House of Representatives (435 members) and the Senate (100 members); function of legislative branch is to make laws; adjective; 4 syllables

✳ **executive**: word used often in social studies; one of the main branches of government, comprising offices of the president, vice-president, cabinet, and agency heads; function is to make sure laws are carried out; adjective; 4 syllables

✳ **phony***: word history—word originated with an imitation gold ring that tricksters sold as real gold. This ring was called "fawney." Around 1920, the word began to be used to mean anything that was fake. The word took on the Greek *ph* rather than the *f*. (Sarnoff & Ruffins, p. 59)

Day 2: Word Combo

Challenge students to complete each sentence with a word that is a combination of word parts from each of the words listed below it. Each word must contain the number of letters beside the sentence. Discuss the meanings of some of the common word parts that students combined to make the new words.

1. The coach will _ _ _ _ _ _ _ _ _ _ _ that move. (11)
   <u>mo</u>nster/<u>de</u>cide/admini<u>strate</u>   (answer: *demonstrate*)

2. Heather is known for her _ _ _ _ _ _ _ _ _ _. (10)
   therm<u>os</u>/ability/<u>gentle</u>/designe<u>r</u>   (answer: *generosity*)

3. Our family enjoys that _ _ _ _ _ _ _ _ _. (9)
   ex<u>tra</u>/con<u>dition</u>   (answer: *tradition*)

4. The cake I baked turned out to be a _ _ _ _ _ _ _ _. (8)
   ranger/<u>dis</u>tinguish/<u>as</u>tronomy   (answer: *disaster*)

5. The garden path is _ _ _ _ _ _ _ _. (8)
   <u>circ</u>umference/do<u>cu</u>ment/stel<u>lar</u>   (answer: *circular*)

Day 3: Word Builder

Have students separate the letters at the bottom of this week's word template. Ask them to spell words as you call them out. Call out words in the order shown below. The final word should answer the following clue: Some of this week's words fit this category. (*congressional*)

loose

loosen

glacier

ignorance

scanner

solace

organ

organic

erosion

gasoline

sign

signal

signaler

assign

reassign

earn

earning

earnings

console

scorn

scorning

censor

encore

enclose

congress

congressional

As students spell each word, write it on the board. Ask them to cross-check their spelling with yours and correct any errors. Discuss any new words and their meanings. Then use the list to brainstorm more words that share a spelling pattern, such as the following:

- *encore*: store, shore, deplore, ignore

- *enclose*: oppose, dispose, close, foreclose, nose

Point out that the word *console* is a heteronym—a word pronounced differently according to its meaning (*console*: "to bring comfort"; *console*: an entertainment cabinet).

Day 4: Linkage

Tell students to see how many words they can find in the chain of letters on the Linkage Word Strips reproducible (page 127). The chain includes weekly words as well as other words. See who can find the most words and discuss the words that students think are interesting. You might ask students to write on the board the most unusual word they found.

Day 5: Word Smart

Ask students to arrange the week's words across the top of their desks with plenty of workspace below. Have them respond to your questions by picking up the correct word card(s) and holding it so you can see the answer. If there are more than two correct answers, tell students to show only two—one in each hand. Ask: *Can you find . . .*

- a word hiding a fruit? (*figure*)
- a word that always begins with a capital letter?
- a word that joins parts of sentences?
- a word that possibly started as a fake ring?
- a word that is a branch of the government?
- a word that rhymes with *sound*?
- words hiding a preposition? (*conjunction, phony*)
- a word for the branch of government that makes laws?
- a word for the branch of government that interprets the laws?
- a word that is a contraction?
- a word for the branch of government that carries out the laws?
- a word that has an /f/ sound?
- a word with 4 syllables?
- a word hiding a word that means "to talk about wildly"? (*travel*)
- a word that names a part of speech?
- a word hiding a body part? (*legislative*)
- a word that often goes with "agent"?
- a word that means "insincere or fake"?
- a word that, if you changed the first two letters to one letter, would be where a pitcher stands?
- a word hiding a place where roads meet? (*conjunction*)
- a word that you use when you are sure about something?
- a word whose vowels mean that someone owes money to someone else?

Now ask students to return the words to the top of their desks. Their next challenge is to sort the words by a common characteristic. Then have partners share their work by asking each other, "What's my rule?" The guesses may include valid categories, but the correct answer must match the partner's rule. Here are some sample categories for this week's words:

- *judicial, legislative, executive* (branches of government)
- *certain, travel, phony, figure* (2 syllables)
- *conjunctions, judicial* (words with a *j*)

Day 1: Meet the Words

Have students pull apart the 10 word cards for this lesson and arrange them across the top of their desks. Then ask students to do the following:

- Hold up each card as you pronounce the word on it.
- Look at the word, read it aloud, and spell it with you.
- Return the word card to the top of their desk.

Provide a definition as necessary and share some of the word's features, as described below.

* **English**: high-frequency word; relates to people, language, and customs originating in England; word history—comes from *Engle* meaning "the Angles," which referred to the group of people who lived on an island shaped like a fish hook (*angle* = "to fish with a hook"); spelled with a capital letter as are references to other countries; 2 syllables

* **finally**: high-frequency word; adverb form as signaled by *-ly* ending; 3 syllables

* **wait**: high-frequency word; usage: noun ("We have a long wait every day for our bus.") and verb ("I will wait with you for the bus."); homophone for *weight*; *ai* makes long-*a* sound

* **correct**: high-frequency word; usage: verb ("The teacher will correct our tests.") and adjective ("That is the correct item."); 2 syllables

* **interjection**: word used often in language arts; part of speech that shows emotion and is characterized by grammatical isolation ("Wow! That was a great pitch!"); some words used as interjections: *Oh! Gee! Stop! Ouch! Yikes!*; in general usage, *interject* means "to add something," as in "Let me interject a comment."; 4 syllables

* **proofread**: word used often in language arts; part of the writing process when a writer reads and marks errors; a person who proofreads is a proofreader; often shortened to *proof*, as in "Will you proof my essay?"; 2 syllables

* **quotations**: word used often in language arts; refers to something that is quoted or taken from another source or sometimes refers to the punctuation marks that show something is being quoted; (*Demonstrate open and closed quotation marks. Show how only exact words are included in quotations*); 3 syllables

* **analogy**: word used often in language arts; refers to the similarity between the features of two things, such as a pump and the heart; analogies are often represented with the use of colons, as in fork : eat : : shovel : dig (Read as "Fork is to eat as shovel is to dig," which means that *fork* and *eat* have the

same relationship as *shovel* and *dig*); -logy in this word does not mean "the study of" but rather refers to logic or reason; 4 syllables

* **alliteration**: word used often in language arts; a figure of speech: several words in a grouping start with the same sound ("Bumblebees buzzed through the bushes."); often used in tongue twisters; can be used in prose or poetry; 5 syllables

* **nightmare***: word history—In 8th century Germany, someone suffering from terrifying dreams was said to be visited by a spirit called Mara or Mera. This spirit could only be banished by binding a knife in a cloth and swinging it around the person three times while chanting. By the 13th century, *Mare* was combined with *night* to form the current compound word *nightmare*. The definition has now broadened to mean any horrendous event. (Flavell & Flavell, 1995)

Day 2: Word Combo

Challenge students to complete each sentence with a word that is a combination of word parts from each of the words listed below it. Each word must contain the number letters given in the sentence. Discuss the meanings of some of the common word parts that students combined to make the new words.

1. Sean needs to be more _ _ _ _ _ _ _ _. (8)
   in<u>ci</u>te/<u>de</u>fect/pas<u>sive</u>   (answer: *decisive*)

2. The student is counting the days until _ _ _ _ _ _ _ _ _ _. (10)
   fl<u>u</u>ctuate/temp<u>tation</u>/<u>grad</u>e   (answer: *graduation*)

3. The hurricane was _ _ _ _ _ _ _ _ _ _. (11)
   con<u>struct</u>/<u>de</u>frost/allus<u>ive</u>   (answer: *destructive*)

4. That baby is _ _ _ _ _ _ _ _! (8)
   <u>pre</u>cede/deli<u>cious</u>   (answer: *precious*)

5. The teacher wants our _ _ _ _ _ _ _ _ _. (9)
   <u>at</u>omic/pre<u>tend</u>/starva<u>tion</u>   (answer: *attention*)

Day 3: Word Builder

Have students separate the letters at the bottom of this week's word template. Ask them to spell words as you call them out. Call out words in the order shown below. The final word should answer the following clue: Words will weave webs of wisdom. (*alliteration*)

tail	oriental
retail	airline
retain	relation
lateral	literal
are	linear
area	alone
arena	loan
alter	roan
altar	ant
ate	rant
eat	tolerant
treat	reliant
orient	alliteration

As students spell each word, write it on the board. Ask them to cross-check their spelling with yours and correct any errors. Then use the list to brainstorm more words that share a spelling pattern, such as the following:

- *alone*: trombone, phone, rhinestone, zone, tone (*-oan* and *-own* may make the same sound)

- *tolerant*: distant, gallant, blatant, fragrant

Day 4: Linkage

Tell students to see how many words they can find in the chain of letters on the Linkage Word Strips reproducible (page 127). The chain includes weekly words as well as other words. See who can find the most words and discuss the words that students think are interesting. You might ask students to write on the board the most unusual word they found.

Day 5: Word Smart

Ask students to arrange the week's words across the top of their desks with plenty of workspace below. Have them respond to your questions by picking up the correct word card(s) and holding it so you can see the answer. If there are more than two correct answers, tell students to show only two—one in each hand. Ask: *Can you find . . .*

- a word hiding a part of a fish? (*finally*)

- a word that is a plural?

- a word hiding something a detective wants? (*proofread*)

- a word with a suffix that signals that it's an adverb?

- a word that is something all good writers do?

- a word that is always capitalized?

- a word that makes most people impatient when they have to do it?

- a word that is often associated with the words of well-known people?

- a word hiding a synonym for *last*? (*finally*)

- a word hiding a part of a house? (*proofread*)

- a word hiding something in a fireplace? (*analogy*)

- a word that, if you added *-er*, would identify someone who works in a restaurant?

- a word that identifies this: "Fish is to swim as birds are to fly"?

- a word with a base that means "to interrupt or to add"?

- a word that can refer to particular punctuation marks?

- a word with the most syllables?

- a word that is a compound?

- a word with only 1 syllable?

- a word that can name a part of speech?

- a word that names a figure of speech?

- a word that originated with a word for a demon or spirit?

- a word that can be used as a verb or an adjective?

Now ask students to return the words to the top of their desks. Their next challenge is to sort the words by a common characteristic. Then have partners share their work by asking each other, "What's my rule?" The guesses may include valid categories, but the correct answer must match the partner's rule. Here are some sample categories for this week's words:

- *finally, quotations* (words with 3 syllables)

- *proofread, nightmare* (compounds)

- *interjection, analogy* (words with 4 syllables)

- *interjection, alliteration, quotations* (same suffix)

Challenge: Complete each analogy.

- *Proofread* is to *correct* as *cure* is to _____. (*heal*)

- *Student* is to *class* as *juror* is to _____. (*jury*)

- *Bat* is to *hit* as *pencil* is to _____. (*write*)

Day 1: Meet the Words

Have students pull apart the 10 word cards for this lesson and arrange them across the top of their desks. Then ask students to do the following:

- Hold up each card as you pronounce the word on it.
- Look at the word, read it aloud, and spell it with you.
- Return the word card to the top of their desk.

Provide a definition as necessary and share some of the word's features, as described below.

* **quickly**: high-frequency word; -ly signals adverb usage; 2 syllables

* **shown**: high-frequency word; verb

* **verb**: high-frequency word used often in language arts; part of speech that shows action or state of being; some verbs are called action verbs, some linking, and some helping; all sentences have subjects and verbs

* **inches**: high-frequency word used often in math; plural form of inch; in math, refers to a measurement, but also has a verb usage ("He slowly inches towards the door."); from Latin uncial, which means "twelfth part" (ask: "What part of a foot is an inch?"); 2 syllables

* **street**: high-frequency word; noun usage; -eet pattern spells many words, such as meet, feet, sweet and makes the same sound as the pattern -eat

* **convex**: word used often in math; in math, means "a polygon with all its interior angles less than or equal to 180 degrees"; in general usage, means "a surface that curves outward"; opposite of concave, which is "a surface that curves inward"; 2 syllables

* **exponent**: word used often in math; means "a symbol placed just to the right above a number to show how many times the number is multiplied by itself"; this process is called raising a number to another power, and the exponent shows the power ($2 \times 2 \times 2 = 8$ can be written as 2^3); in general usage, something that multiplies or grows quickly may be referred to as growing exponentially; 3 syllables

* **parallelogram**: word used often in math; means "a quadrilateral with both pairs of opposite sides parallel to each other" (draw parallelogram); a rectangle is a parallelogram; parallel means "lines that are equal distance from each other at all points"; word part para is Greek and means "side by side" or "beside"; word part gram means "written or drawn"; 5 syllables

* **vertex**: word used often in math; in math, means "the point common to three or more sides of a geometric solid (such as a pyramid)"; in general usage, means "the highest point or summit"; 2 syllables

* **nickname***: word history—In England in the 1200s, many people had the same given name, and few family names were used, so finding the right William was often difficult. Many people assumed an ekename, a word meaning "also or other." Ekename gradually evolved into nickname. (Sarnoff & Ruffins, p. 31)

Day 2: Word Combo

Challenge students to complete each sentence with a word that is a combination of word parts from each of the words listed below it. Each word must contain the number of letters beside the sentence. Discuss the meanings of some of the common word parts that students combined to make the new words.

1. Can you make a _ _ _ _ _ _ _ _ _ _? (10)
   dictate/pretender/revolution   (answer: prediction)

2. Molly worked hard for her _ _ _ _ _ _ _ _ _. (9)
   indication/progress/motive   (answer: promotion)

3. Cal's _ _ _ _ _ _ _ _ _ _ _ _ _ _ occurred after his graduation. (14)
   citation/formulate/translate   (answer: transformation)

4. We followed the _ _ _ _ _ _ _ _ path of the birds. (9)
   microscope/grateful/creation   (answer: migration)

5. The marathon runner had _ _ _ _ _ _ _ _ _. (9)
   duration/enclosure/insurance   (answer: endurance)

Day 3: Word Builder

Have students separate the letters at the bottom of this week's word template. Ask them to spell words as you call them out. Call out words in the order shown below. The final word should answer the following clue: Squares and rectangles can be classified as this. (parallelogram)

armor

alarm

regal

gallop

gleam

glare

galore

moral

llama

legal

regal

game

program

polar

pearl

parole

rampage

parallel

parallelogram

As students spell each word, write it on the board. Ask them to cross-check their spelling with yours and correct any errors. Discuss any new words and their meanings. Then use the list to brainstorm more words that share a spelling pattern, such as the following:

- *game*: shame, frame, nickname, pregame, enflame

- *parole*: hole, mole, stole, cajole, flagpole

Day 4: Linkage

Tell students to see how many words they can find in the chain of letters on the Linkage Word Strips reproducible (page 127). The chain includes weekly words as well as other words. See who can find the most words and discuss the words that students think are interesting. You might ask students to write on the board the most unusual word they found.

Day 5: Word Smart

Ask students to arrange the week's words across the top of their desks with plenty of workspace below. Have them respond to your questions by picking up the correct word card(s) and holding it so you can see the answer. If there are more than two correct answers, tell students to show only two—one in each hand. Ask: *Can you find . . .*

- a word that refers to a measurement?

- a word hiding a question word? (*shown*)

- a word with a word part that means "written or drawn"?

- a word with a suffix that makes it an adverb?

- a word that goes with the word *subject*?

- a word that ends with a vowel?

- a word that refers to a math symbol?

- a word that helps describe action?

- a word with a pair of vowels next to each other?

- a word with 5 syllables?

- a word that ends with a letter pair often used as prefixes?

- a word with a word part that means "side by side" or "beside"?

- a word that rhymes with *greet*?

- a word that turns *Anthony* into *Tony*?

- a word that means "the highest point"?

- a word that refers to shapes?

- a word that means "the number of times a number is multiplied by itself"?

- a word hiding a word that means "to present or display"? (*shown*)

- a word that is the opposite of *concave*?

Now ask students to return the words to the top of their desks. Their next challenge is to sort the words by a common characteristic. Then have partners share their work by asking each other, "What's my rule?" The guesses may include valid categories, but the correct answer must match the partner's rule. Here are some sample categories for this week's words:

- *convex, exponent, parallelogram, vertex, inches* (math terms)

- *shown, verb, exponent* (words that have consonants as the last 2 letters)

- *verb, shown* (one word is an example of the other)

- *verb, vertex* (words that start with *v*)

- *street, exponent, vertex* (words with 2 *e*'s)

Day 1: Meet the Words

Have students pull apart the 10 word cards for this lesson and arrange them across the top of their desks. Then ask students to do the following:

- Hold up each card as you pronounce the word on it.
- Look at the word, read it aloud, and spell it with you.
- Return the word card to the top of their desk.

Provide a definition as necessary and share some of the word's features, as described below.

* **decided**: high-frequency word; past tense of *decide*; 3 syllables

* **course**: high-frequency word; multiple meanings, some of which are 1) "a direction taken," 2) "a program of study," and 3) "a part of a meal served at one time"; homophone for *coarse* (rough); tricky spelling with *ou* vowel combination

* **surface**: high-frequency word; noun usage means "the outside or exterior of something" ("The surface of the shelf is smooth."); verb usage means "to come to the top" ("Jacques held his breath until he was able to surface."); word part *sur* comes from French word meaning "above" (*above* + *face*)

* **produce**: high-frequency word; heteronym (words with same spelling but different meanings and pronunciations); different meanings: *produce* (with stress on first syllable) means "something that is produced" or "agricultural products," *produce* (with stress on last syllable) means "to make, manufacture, or bring into existence"; other examples of heteronyms: *bow* (and arrow) or *bow* (bend at the waist); *lead* (to give direction) or *lead* (metal); 2 syllables

* **potential**: word used often in science to name one of the two forms of energy–stored energy; also general usage as adjective ("Vince is a potential quarterback.") and as a noun ("The cocker spaniel shows a lot of potential."); 3 syllables

* **kinetic**: word used often in science to name one of the two forms of energy–working energy; comes from the Greek word *kinein* meaning "move"– *cinema* is also originated from *kinein*; 3 syllables

* **chemical**: word used often in science for potential energy in which energy is stored in the bonds of atoms and molecules (example: The petroleum used in cars is chemical energy that becomes thermal energy when it's burned in the engine and makes the car move.); general use refers to a substance made through a chemical process; related to *chemistry*, *chemist*; 3 syllables

* **thermal**: word used often in science for one form of kinetic energy in which molecules move faster and faster as they are heated (example: a log burning in the fireplace or a pot boiling on the stove); general use refers to heat as in *thermos*, *thermometer*; word part *therm* means "heat"; 2 syllables

* **mechanical**: word used often in science for one form of kinetic energy in which energy is stored in an object by tension (example: a stretched rubber band or a compressed spring); in general use, having to do with machinery; 4 syllables

* **crazy***: word history–The earliest use of the word (15th century) meant "full of cracks." A crazy boat was one in danger of sinking if it weren't repaired. In the 17th century, the word began to be used in reference to people, usually as an insult. (Sarnoff & Ruffins, p. 20)

Day 2: Word Combo

Challenge students to complete each sentence with a word that is a combination of word parts from each of the words listed below it. Each word must contain the number of letters given in the sentence. Discuss the meanings of some of the common word parts that students combined to make the new words.

1. Sasha's father is very _ _ _ _ _ _ _ _ _ in the community. (9)
   <u>inter</u>ested/<u>prom</u>/par<u>ental</u>   (answer: *prominent*)

2. Freezing makes the fish _ _ _ _ _ _ _ _ _ _. (10)
   im<u>port</u>ed/<u>ex</u>ited/teach<u>able</u>   (answer: *exportable*)

3. The bread is _ _ _ _ _ _ _ _ _ _. (10)
   comfor<u>table</u>/<u>peri</u>scope/standoff<u>ish</u>   (answer: *perishable*)

4. What I'm saying is _ _ _ _ _ _ _ _ _ _ _ _. (12)
   presi<u>dential</u>/<u>offi</u>cial/<u>confi</u>ding   (answer: *confidential*)

5. The document proved their _ _ _ _ _ _ _ _ _ _ _ _. (12)
   friend<u>ship</u>/<u>guard</u>ed/meri<u>dian</u>   (answer: *guardianship*)

Day 3: Word Builder

Have students separate the letters at the bottom of this week's word template. Ask them to spell words as you call them out. Call out words in the order shown below. The final word should answer the following clue: These might measure the sun's rays and your brother Ray's fever. (*thermometers*)

remote

tremor

mothers

smother

terms

themes

three

storm

short

shorter

sheet

teeth

there

other

meters

meteors

resort

thermos

thermometers

As students spell each word, write it on the board. Ask them to cross-check their spelling with yours and correct any errors. Then use the list to brainstorm more words that share a spelling pattern, such as the following:

- *remote*: devote, note, promote, vote, wrote (-oat makes the same sound)

- *storm*: reform, conform, transform, rainstorm

Day 4: Linkage

Tell students to see how many words they can find in the chain of letters on the Linkage Word Strips reproducible (page 127). The chain includes weekly words as well as other words. See who can find the most words and discuss the words that students think are interesting. You might ask students to write on the board the most unusual word they found.

Day 5: Word Smart

Ask students to arrange the week's words across the top of their desks with plenty of workspace below. Have them respond to your questions by picking up the correct word card(s) and holding it so you can see the answer. If there are more than two correct answers, tell students to show only two—one in each hand. Ask: *Can you find . . .*

- a word that contains a pronoun other than *I*? (*chemical, thermal, mechanical*)

- a word hiding someone who works on cars? (*mechanical*)

- a word that has a word part that means "heat"?

- a word that names the two types of energy?

- a word that is a synonym for *capability*?

- a word for a type of energy that is stored?

- a word for type of energy that works?

- a word that originated with cracks?

- a word pronounced two different ways depending on its meaning?

- a word that names a form of energy represented by a moving car?

- a word for a form of energy represented by a burning fire?

- a word for a form of energy represented by a turbine powering conveyor belts?

- a word for a form of energy represented by a stretched rubber band?

- a word that fits in this sentence: "I'm taking a _____ in American literature."?

- a word that fits in this sentence: "The first _____ is a salad."?

- a word that fits in this sentence: "We hope to _____ a play this year."?

- a word that fits in this sentence: "We stored the _____ in the refrigerator until dinner."?

- a word that solves this analogy: chemical : potential : : _____ : kinetic?

- a word that fits in this sentence: "We live on the earth's crust, which is its _____."?

- a word in the past tense?

- a word hiding the abbreviation of the last month? (*decided*)

- a word hiding a water sport? (*surface*)

- a word hiding something you cook in? (*potential*)

- a word hiding something that is a part of your head? (*surface*)

Now ask students to return the words to the top of their desks. Their next challenge is to sort the words by a common characteristic. Then have partners share their work by asking each other, "What's my rule?" The guesses may include valid categories, but the correct answer must match the partner's rule. Here are some sample categories for this week's words:

- *potential, kinetic* (the two types of energy)

- *thermal, chemical, mechanical* (some of the forms of energy)

- *thermal, mechanical* (forms of kinetic energy)

- *course, thermal, mechanical* (words hiding pronouns)

- *decided, potential, kinetic, chemical, mechanical* (words with more than 2 syllables)

Day 1: Meet the Words

Have students pull apart the 10 word cards for this lesson and arrange them across the top of their desks. Then ask students to do the following:

- Hold up each card as you pronounce the word on it.
- Look at the word, read it aloud, and spell it with you.
- Return the word card to the top of their desk.

Provide a definition as necessary and share some of the word's features, as described below.

* **yet**: frequently used word; adverb ("Don't leave yet!") and conjunction ("I made a good grade, yet I could have done better.")

* **government**: frequently used word; -ment suffix changes verb govern into a noun; 3 syllables

* **object**: frequently used word; heteronym (words with same spelling but different origins, meanings, and pronunciations); with stress on first syllable, means "something tangible" (noun); with stress on second syllable, means "to offer an argument or reason for being opposed to something" (verb); 2 syllables

* **among**: frequently used word; preposition ("This letter was among my papers."); 2 syllables

* **cannot**: frequently used word; sometimes written as two separate words, which is also correct

* **revenue**: word used often in social studies; means "the income of a government from taxes and other sources"; tricky ending sounds like new; 3 syllables

* **annex**: word used often in social studies; (verb) "to attach to something larger, such as a city, by annexing an adjoining area and increasing its size"; (noun) "something that is added to a larger body, such as an emergency annex of a hospital"; 2 syllables

* **boycott***: word used often in social studies; verb usage means "to stop dealing with" as when an animal rights organization encourages customers to boycott meat products; noun usage is the act of boycotting as in, "The boycott caused the restaurant to close."; 2 syllables; word history—A ruthless Englishman, Charles C. Boycott (1832–97), evicted tenants from his properties. The tenants decided to refuse to cooperate with Boycott and his family. This nonviolent tactic grew in popularity because it was effective. *Note*: A word derived from the name of a person is called an *eponym*.

* **immigrant**: word used often in social studies; "a person who comes to one country from another"; related to *migrate* ("to move"); 3 syllables

* **paragraph***: word history—The ancient Greeks wrote their manuscripts by hand. Because paper was so valuable, they left no space for a paragraph, but they put a mark to show the beginning of a new topic. The mark was a combination of *para*, meaning "by the side" and *graph*, meaning "to write." When a space was later included, the word *paragraph* was used for the text between the spaces. (Sarnoff & Ruffins, p. 52)

Day 2: Word Combo

Challenge students to complete each sentence with a word that is a combination of word parts from each of the words listed below it. Each word must contain the number of letters given in the sentence. Discuss the meanings of some of the common word parts that students combined to make the new words.

1. Do you want to _ _ _ _ _ _ _ _ _ to the bake sale? (10)
   pollute/congruent/tribulation   (answer: *contribute*)

2. We are going to fix that problem _ _ _ _ _ _ _ _ _. (9)
   recently/stanza/herein   (answer: *instantly*)

3. The sunset was the artist's _ _ _ _ _ _ _ _ _ _ _. (11)
   spiral/injury/temptation   (answer: *inspiration*)

4. The noise was _ _ _ _ _ _ _ _ _ _ _. (11)
   contract/district/dancing   (answer: *distracting*)

5. _ _ _ _ _ _ _ _ _ _ _ _ _ _ _ on winning! (15)
   gratuity/concave/relations   (answer: *congratulations*)

Day 3: Word Builder

Have students separate the letters at the bottom of this week's word template. Ask them to spell words as you call them out. Call out words in the order shown below. The final word should answer the following clue: You go through this process when you enter a country. (*immigration*)

roam

roaming

riot

trio

omit

amigo

gator

goat

maim

maiming

tiring

timing

atom

margin

rain

grain

gram

ratio

migration

immigration

As students spell each word, write it on the board. Ask them to cross-check their spelling with yours and correct any errors. Then use the list to brainstorm more words that share a spelling pattern, such as the following:

- *goat*: boat, float, moat, bloat, coat, oat (-*ote* makes the same sound)

- *grain*: rain, drain, detain, regain, retain

Day 4: Linkage

Tell students to see how many words they can find in the chain of letters on the Linkage Word Strips reproducible (page 127). The chain includes weekly words as well as other words. See who can find the most words and discuss the words that students think are interesting. You might ask students to write on the board the most unusual word they found.

Day 5: Word Smart

Ask students to arrange the week's words across the top of their desks with plenty of workspace below. Have them respond to your questions by picking up the correct word card(s) and holding it so you can see the answer. If there are more than two correct answers, tell students to show only two—one in each hand. Ask: *Can you find . . .*

- a word that is a conjunction?

- a word hiding a group of males? (*govern*ment)

- a word that derives from a man's name?

- a word sometimes written as two words?

- a word hiding something you might sleep on? (*boy*cott)

- a word that is a synonym for *income*?

- a word that means "a person who moves to one country from another"?

- a word with a suffix that changes it from a verb to a noun?

- a word hiding an insect? (*immig*rant)

- a word hiding the opposite of *odd*? (*reven*ue)

- a word hiding the abbreviation for a day of the week? (*among*)

- a word hiding something a fairy godmother may do to your wishes? (*immigrant*)

- a word that is a preposition?

- a word that is an antonym for *can*?

- a word that means "adding something to something larger"?

- a word that means "to resist something, usually because of principles"?

- a word that relates to the grouping of topics?

- a word that is a heteronym–pronounced two ways depending on its meaning?

- a word that fits in this sentence: "The state's main source of _____ is tourism."?

- a word hiding a person who moves regularly, often to find work? (*immigrant*)

- a word with a word part that refers to something written or drawn? (*paragraph*)

Now ask students to return the words to the top of their desks. Their next challenge is to sort the words by a common characteristic. Then have partners share their work by asking each other, "What's my rule?" The guesses may include valid categories, but the correct answer must match the partner's rule. Here are some sample categories for this week's words:

- *annex, boycott, immigrant, cannot* (words with double consonants)

- *revenue* (only word ending in a vowel)

- *government, revenue, immigrant, paragraph* (3 syllables)

- *yet* (only word with 1 syllable)

Day 1: Meet the Words

Have students pull apart the 10 word cards for this lesson and arrange them across the top of their desks. Then ask students to do the following:

- Hold up each card as you pronounce the word on it.
- Look at the word, read it aloud, and spell it with you.
- Return the word card to the top of their desk.

Provide a definition as necessary and share some of the word's features, as described below.

* **machine**: frequently used word; means "a device that modifies force or motion"; 2 syllables

* **plane**: frequently used word; multiple meanings: 1) "an aircraft" or 2) "a flat or level surface"

* **system**: frequently used word; means "a combination of things or parts that form a complex whole"; 2 syllables

* **brought**: frequently used word; past tense of *bring*; tricky spelling with *-ought* pattern; spelling pattern helps with words like *fought, ought, thought, sought*

* **understand**: frequently used word; means "to grasp meaning"; 3 syllables

* **hyperbole**: word used often in language arts; a figure of speech in which exaggeration is used for emphasis and effect ("The ride home took forever." "That casserole could feed an army!"); general usage shortens this to *hype* as in exaggerated sports stories; 4 syllables

* **idiom**: word used often in language arts; a form of expression that is not literal but is figurative or similar to a metaphor ("It's raining cats and dogs." "You're pulling my leg." "The test was a piece of cake!"); 3 syllables

* **superlative**: word used often in language arts; the highest degree of comparison among adjectives and adverbs, such as *tall/tallest; good/best, carefully/most carefully*; in general usage, it means "the highest degree or quality" or "outstanding," such as, "He is a superlative athlete."; 4 syllables

* **clause**: word used often in language arts; a subject and predicate that form either a complete simple sentence or part of a sentence; three types of clauses: independent or main ("Because the student is new, he will need help catching up." Or "He will need help catching up."), dependent or subordinate ("Because the student is new, he will need help catching up."), and coordinate clause ("The student is new,

and he will need help catching up."); in general usage, "an article in a legal document"

* **quarantine***: means "to suspend travel or communication" (Often, astronauts are quarantined when they first return from space, which means they are separated from others for a specified amount of time.); word history—The word comes from the French word *quarante*, which means "forty." When a ship arriving in a port was suspected of carrying crew members with a contagious disease, it was kept offshore and out of contact for about forty days. *Quarantine* came to be the term for any such imposed isolation. (Flavell & Flavell, pp. 199–200)

Day 2: Word Combo

Challenge students to complete each sentence with a word that is a combination of word parts from each of the words listed below it. Each word must contain the number of letters given in the sentence. Discuss the meanings of some of the common word parts that students combined to make the new words.

1. Did that happen _ _ _ _ _ _ _ _? (8)
   de<u>cent</u>/re<u>gain</u>/sincere<u>ly</u>   (answer: *recently*)

2. There was some _ _ _ _ _ _ _ _ _ about where we were going to meet. (9)
   fugitive/<u>con</u>vincing/percu<u>ssion</u>   (answer: *confusion*)

3. The soldiers were kept in _ _ _ _ _ _ _ _ _. (9)
   re<u>cap</u>/ac<u>tiv</u>e/gra<u>vity</u>   (answer: *captivity*)

4. The car was difficult to _ _ _ _ _ _ _ _ in the rain. (8)
   <u>man</u>date/n<u>eu</u>tral/fe<u>ver</u>ish   (answer: *maneuver*)

5. The help came _ _ _ _ _ _ _ _ _ _ late. (10)
   ma<u>g</u>ic/<u>tra</u>dition/stoi<u>cally</u>   (answer: *tragically*)

Day 3: Word Builder

Have students separate the letters at the bottom of this week's word template. Ask them to spell words as you call them out. Call out words in the order shown below. The final word should answer the following clue: These are always the best part of job well done. (*superlatives*)

relate

relatives

reveal

several

leaves

lapse

prevail

private

erupt

rustle

virus

viruses

values

stripe

strive

sprite

priest

pasture

virtual

versatile

travel

super

superlatives

As students spell each word, write it on the board. Ask them to cross-check their spelling with yours and correct any errors. Then use the list to brainstorm more words that share a spelling pattern, such as the following:

- *relate*: hate, fate, gate, estate, frustrate (-*eight* and –*ait* make the same sound)

- *reveal*: appeal, real, ideal, heal, repeal, zeal (-*eel* makes the same sound)

Day 4: Linkage

Tell students to see how many words they can find in the chain of letters on the Linkage Word Strips reproducible (page 127). The chain includes weekly words as well as other words. See who can find the most words and discuss the words that students think are interesting. You might ask students to write on the board the most unusual word they found.

Day 5: Word Smart

Ask students to arrange the week's words across the top of their desks with plenty of workspace below. Have them respond to your questions by picking up the correct word card(s) and holding it so you can see the answer. If there are more than two correct

answers, tell students to show only two—one in each hand. Ask: *Can you find . . .*

- a word hiding a narrow passageway? (*plane*)

- a word that is a figure of speech that involves exaggeration?

- a word that is a synonym for *outstanding*?

- a word represented by the words *tallest, smallest, bravest*?

- a word hiding a preposition that is the opposite of *over*? (*understand*)

- a word that means "parts organized into a whole"?

- a word that could refer to a mode of transportation?

- a word hiding a word that is the opposite of *sit*? (*understand*)

- a word that, if the last letter were changed, would refer to a foolish person?

- a word that can mean "a flat surface"?

- a word that relates to the phrase "about forty"?

- a word represented by a pulley, a car, a vacuum, or a dishwasher?

- a word that names an expression that is not meant to be literal?

- a word that can refer to an article in a legal document?

- a word that can contain a subject and predicate?

- a word that rhymes with *thought*?

- a word that describes our sun, the planets, and stars?

- a word hiding a word used to describe someone who is very active? (*hyperbole*)

- a word hiding an action word? (*quarantine*)

- a word hiding something you would like written on your test? (*superlative*)

- a word that sounds like something a lobster has?

- a word that is a synonym for *sequester* or *hold separately*?

- a word that means "to grasp meaning"?

Ask students to identify the word that each example represents:

- Dad blew his top when he saw how much it cost! (*idiom*)

- I'm so hungry I could eat a horse! (*hyperbole*)

- *biggest, fastest, reddest, highest, worst* (*superlatives*)

- I could sleep for days! (*hyperbole*)

- He ran as fast as a cheetah. (*hyperbole*)

- I was so happy, I was walking on air. (*idiom*)

- *generator, refrigerator, air conditioner, pump* (*machine*)

Day 1: Meet the Words

Have students pull apart the 10 word cards for this lesson and arrange them across the top of their desks. Then ask students to do the following:

- Hold up each card as you pronounce the word on it.
- Look at the word, read it aloud, and spell it with you.
- Return the word card to the top of their desk.

Provide a definition as necessary and share some of the word's features, as described below.

✻ **explain**: high-frequency word; used often in all academic areas; synonym for *say* or *tell*; 2 syllables

✻ **though**: high-frequency word; commonly misspelled because -ough making long-*o* sound; sometimes confused with *thought* and *through*; used as conjunction ("Though she had always been shy, she sang well on the stage.") and as adverb ("I don't know if we can go, though.")

✻ **language**: high-frequency word; general academic word; tricky spelling with *ua*; derived from Latin word *langue*, which means "tongue"; 2 syllables

✻ **thousands**: high-frequency word; plural; singular *thousand* is cardinal number represented by 1,000 and Roman numeral M; 2 syllables

✻ **equation**: word used often in math; means "an expression that represents equal quantities, such as $3 + 5 = 1 + 7$"; some equations are written with letters that represent unknown quantities: $3 + b = 1 + 7$

✻ **inequality**: word used often in math; means "a statement or equation that proves its parts are not equal"; often represented in equations with the symbols $\neq$ (inequality), $<$ (less than), $>$ (greater than); also used in social studies and general usage to describe social conditions that are unequal or unjust; prefix *in-* means "not"; suffix *-ity* means "state or quality of"; 5 syllables

✻ **ratio**: word used often in math; means "a comparison of two numbers"; (example: if there are 20 boys and 10 girls, the ratio of boys to girls is 2 to 1—also written as 2:1 or 2/1); 2 syllables

✻ **volume**: word used often in math; multiple meanings: 1) "the amount of space that matter occupies," 2) "one book of a set," 3) "the degree of sound," or 4) "a large quantity"; 2 syllables

✻ **equilateral**: word used often in math; means "having all sides equal," as in an equilateral triangle (*draw one*); word part *equi* means "equal"; 5 syllables

✻ **digits**✻: word history—The numbers 0–9 are referred to as digits, which comes from the Latin word *digitus* meaning "finger." This word was probably used because people often count on their fingers. (Sarnoff & Ruffins, p. 33)

Day 2: Word Combo

Challenge students to complete each sentence with a word that is a combination of word parts from each of the words listed below it. Each word must contain the number of letters given in the sentence. Discuss the meanings of some of the common word parts that students combined to make the new words.

1. Helen's _ _ _ _ _ _ _ _ _ _ _ _ skill was amazing! (12)
   seismo<u>graph</u>/<u>photo</u>synthesis/comi<u>cal</u>   (answer: *photographic*)

2. The food was _ _ _ _ _ _ _. (7)
   gangly/athle<u>tic</u>/<u>ori</u>ental   (answer: *organic*)

3. Max built up _ _ _ _ _ _ _ _ over the years. (8)
   am<u>mu</u>nition/responsibil<u>ity</u>/<u>im</u>portant   (answer: *immunity*)

4. The disease was in the dog's _ _ _ _ _ _ _ _ _. (9)
   con<u>test</u>ant/<u>in</u>decent/mar<u>ine</u>   (answer: *intestine*)

5. The prank caused the student's _ _ _ _ _ _ _ _ _ _. (10)
   ex<u>pen</u>sive/<u>sus</u>pect/man<u>sion</u>   (answer: *suspension*)

Day 3: Word Builder

Have students separate the letters at the bottom of this week's word template. Ask them to spell words as you call them out. Call out words in the order shown below. The final word should answer the following clue: Each side of this type of triangle has something in common. (*equilateral*)

equal

equate

quart

tile

tiler

quilt

quilter

quit

quiet

quite

alert

later

trial

retail

tell

retell

teller

true

area

tire

irate

equilateral

As students spell each word, write it on the board. Ask them to cross-check their spelling with yours and correct any errors. Discuss any new words and their meanings. Then use the list to brainstorm more words that share a spelling pattern, such as the following:

- *retell*: stairwell, farewell, misspell, befell

- *tire*: perspire, entire, haywire, acquire, expire

Stress the difference in the set of words: *quit/quiet/quite* as they are frequently misspelled. Review some of the prefixes and suffixes and how they change word meanings, such as *quilt/quilter, tile/tiler, tell/retell*.

Day 4: Linkage

Tell students to see how many words they can find in the chain of letters on the Linkage Word Strips reproducible (page 127). The chain includes weekly words, as well as other words. See who can find the most words and discuss the words that students think are interesting. You might ask students to write on the board the most unusual word they found.

Day 5: Word Smart

Ask students to arrange the week's words across the top of their desks with plenty of workspace below. Have them respond to your questions by picking up the correct word card(s) and holding it so you can see the answer. If there are more than two correct answers, tell students to show only two—one in each hand. Ask: *Can you find . . .*

- a word hiding a rodent? (*ratio*)

- words sharing the same word part that means "same as"?

- a word that refers to what your parents might ask you to

turn down?

- a word that can refer to numbers or to people's rights?

- a word hiding the antonym for *early*? (*equilateral*)

- a word hiding the opposite of *fancy*? (*explain*)

- a word that is plural?

- a word that might refer to English, Urdu, Spanish, or Tagalog?

- a word that compares?

- a word hiding what you did to your supper last night? (*equilateral*)

- a word that could name a measurement or a book in a set?

- a word that is a verb?

- a word that may be represented by ≠?

- a word that may be represented as 5:2?

- a word hiding something we measure in years? (*language*)

- a word that names something that might be measured in cups, ounces, or liters?

- a word hiding something you might find at the beach? (*thousands*)

- a word hiding what is done in a mine? (*digits*)

- a word that has only 2 sounds?

- a word with the most syllables?

- a word with the fewest syllables?

- a word with a prefix that means "not"?

Now ask students to return the words to the top of their desks. Their next challenge is to sort the words by a common characteristic. Then have partners share their work by asking each other, "What's my rule?" The guesses may include valid categories, but the correct answer is the partner's rule. Here are some sample categories for this week's words:

- *explain, equation, equilateral* (words that start with a vowel)

- *equation, inequality, equilateral* (words that have a word part that means "equal or same")

- *thousands, equation, inequality, ratio, volume, equilateral, digits* (words that relate to numbers)

- *though, thousands* (words that have 2 of the same consonant)

- *explain, language, thousands, equation, inequality, ratio, volume, equilateral* (words that each have 3 different vowels)

Day 1: Meet the Words

Have students pull apart the 10 word cards for this lesson and arrange them across the top of their desks. Then ask students to do the following:

- Hold up each card as you pronounce the word on it.
- Look at the word, read it aloud, and spell it with you.
- Return the word card to the top of their desk.

Provide a definition as necessary and share some of the word's features, as described below.

✻ **carefully**: frequently used word; adverb usage as signaled by -ly ending; -ful suffix means "full of"; synonyms are watchfully and cautiously; 3 syllables

✻ **scientists**: frequently used word that is often misspelled; plural; means "experts in the field of science"; 3 syllables

✻ **known**: frequently used word; related to know and knowledge; -own spelling pattern helps spell words like blown, sown, own; silent k

✻ **island**: frequently used word; "a mass of land surrounded by water and too small to be a continent"; long-i sound and tricky silent s; 2 syllables

✻ **constellation**: word used often in science; means "a group of stars to which names have been given" (examples: Big Dipper, Orion, Ursa Major); constellations are studied by astronomers; 4 syllables

✻ **eclipse**: word used often in science; 2 types of eclipses: 1) a lunar eclipse occurs when the earth comes between the sun and the moon causing a shadow to fall on the moon and 2) a solar eclipse occurs when the moon comes between the earth and the sun, blocking out the sun's rays; also everyday usage as verb meaning "to make something less outstanding," as in "When she sang 'The Star Spangled Banner' so beautifully, she eclipsed the whole first half of the game!"; 2 syllables

✻ **cholesterol**: word used often in science and health; means "a waxy substance produced by the liver which is used to form cell membranes and some hormones"; high levels of cholesterol are associated with heart disease; most vegetables, fruits, and grains do not contain cholesterol, but animal products do contain it, such as meat, egg yolks, and dairy products; 4 syllables

✻ **carcinogen**: word used often in science and health; means "any substance that tends to produce a type of cancer"; some known carcinogens include tobacco, asbestos, second-hand smoke, radon; 4 syllables

✻ **translucent**: word used often in science; means "permitting light to pass through but diffusing it" (example: frosted glass); word part trans means "across or through"; word part lucent comes from Latin lucere, which means "to shine"; 3 syllables

✻ **husband***: word history—Word comes from Old English words hus, from which we got the word house, and from bondi, which means "owner." Original meaning referred to those who owned houses or who were heads of their households and who were called husbands. Now the word is applied to all married men. (Sarnoff & Ruffins, p. 15)

Day 2: Word Combo

Challenge students to complete each sentence with a word that is a combination of word parts from each of the words listed below it. Each word must contain the number of letters given in the sentence. Discuss the meanings of some of the common word parts that students combined to make the new words.

1. He didn't want the trailer set up on his _ _ _ _ _ _ _ _. (8)
   beau<u>ty</u>/<u>pro</u>bably/per<u>tinent</u>   (answer: property)

2. The scientist had to _ _ _ _ _ _ _ _ the bacteria. (8)
   def<u>la</u>te/<u>in</u>side/<u>cub</u>ical   (answer: incubate)

3. It's cold, but they keep turning down the _ _ _ _ _ _ _ _ _ _. (10)
   sta<u>t</u>ic/<u>mo</u>tionless/<u>ther</u>mal   (answer: thermostat)

4. We need to have greater _ _ _ _ _ _ _ _ _. (9)
   avoi<u>dance</u>/<u>to</u>matoes/holle<u>r</u>ing   (answer: tolerance)

5. The idea was met with _ _ _ _ _ _ _ _ _ _. (10)
   per<u>sist</u>/frag<u>rance</u>/<u>re</u>entry   (answer: resistance)

Day 3: Word Builder

Have students separate the letters at the bottom of this week's word template. Ask them to spell words as you call them out. Call out words in the order shown below. The final word should answer the following clue: If your cholesterol is high, you'll have to watch out for this type of disease. (cardiovascular)

card

cardiac

radical

racial

carload

visor

visual

ocular

our

scour

rascal

avoid

radar

vocal

occur

crucial

rural

advisor

viral

rival

vascular

cardiovascular

As students spell each word, write it on the board. Ask them to cross-check their spelling with yours and correct any errors. Discuss any new words and their meanings.

Then explore the similarities and differences among the words *visor*, *visual*, and *ocular*. Look at the word part *cardio* and think of words that contain it, such as *cardiologist, cardiogram, cardiovascular*, and *cardio* workout. Discuss how the meaning of *cardio* relates to those words. Ask: *When someone goes to the gym and does a cardio routine, what are they improving?*

Day 4: Word Action

To each pair or small group, give one of this week's words or allow them to choose the word. Ask them to either plan a short skit or write a short skit to demonstrate the word. Caution students not to use the word in their skits. Ask pairs or groups to read or perform their skits to see if the rest of the class can guess the word. Because several words are similar in meaning, be sure to discuss any guesses that don't match the writers' word but could possibly be acceptable.

Day 5: Word Smart

Ask students to arrange the week's words across the top of their desks with plenty of workspace below. Have them respond to

your questions by picking up the correct word card(s) and holding it so you can see the answer. If there are more than two correct answers, tell students to show only two—one in each hand. Ask: *Can you find . . .*

- a word that names a certain group of people?
- a word hiding something that may be used to bind things together? (*ec*lip*se, hus*band)
- a word hiding a mode of transportation? (*car*efully)
- a word hiding a small amount of money? (*translu*cent)
- a word with a silent *s*?
- a word with a silent *h*?
- a word that has 4 syllables?
- a word that originated from *house*?
- a word that may refer to the Big Dipper, the Little Dipper, or Orion?
- a word that names something you don't want a lot of in your body?
- a word with an ending that signals that it is an adverb?
- a word associated with cancer?
- a word that can be lunar or solar?
- a word hiding the partner of *then*? (*kn*own)
- a word that is plural?
- a word hiding a word that means "to possess something"? (*kn*own)
- a word hiding a part of your face? (*ec*lip*se*)
- a word that describes a material that diffuses light as it passes through?
- a word represented by tobacco or asbestos?
- a word that helps build cell membranes (you need the good kind but not the bad kind)?
- a word hiding a group with instruments? (*hus*band)
- a word for Bermuda, Iceland, or Fiji?

Now ask students to return the words to the top of their desks. Their next challenge is to sort the words by a common characteristic. Then have partners share their work by asking each other, "What's my rule?" The guesses may include valid categories, but the correct answer is the partner's rule. Here are some sample categories for this week's words:

- *cholesterol, carcinogen* (things bad for your health—note that there is "good" cholesterol as well)
- *scientists, husband* (words that name people)
- *known, island, cholesterol* (words with silent letters)
- *carefully, scientists, translucent* (words with 3 syllables)

Day 1: Meet the Words

Note: This is the first week that the words have a connecting theme: words that express degrees of anger and hostility. These words are good for students to know in order to express their own feelings. Some words differ only slightly in degree, while others show a huge difference of emotion. Don't worry about your students' grasping the smallest nuances of difference. Having a general knowledge of these words will be helpful. Begin by discussing the words and whether students have heard them before and in which contexts.

Have students pull apart the 10 word cards for this lesson and arrange them across the top of their desks. Then ask students to do the following:

- Hold up each card as you pronounce the word on it.
- Look at the word, read it aloud, and spell it with you.
- Return the word card to the top of their desk.

Provide a definition as necessary and share some of the word's features, as described below.

∗ *hostile*: means "aggressive and warlike"; originated with Latin *hostis* meaning enemy; related to *hostage*; homophone of *hostel*, which is a safe, inexpensive place to stay when traveling; 2 syllables

∗ *aggravated*: means "annoyed"; different, more serious meaning in legal terms as in, *aggravated assault*; 4 syllables

∗ *belligerent*: means "aggressively hostile and combative"; originated with Latin *belligerare*, which means "to wage war"; 4 syllables

∗ *arrogant*: means "making claims or giving the appearance of superior importance"; synonym is *haughty*; antonyms are *meek* and *modest*; 3 syllables

∗ *callous*: means "hardened and unfeeling"; related to a callus that might develop on a foot after a shoe has rubbed the skin continually (discuss how the meanings are related; from the Latin word *callosus*, which means "thick-skinned"; 2 syllables

∗ *obnoxious*: means "offensive, annoying"; often said of show-off behavior that draws attention; notice word part *noxious*, which means "harmful and injurious," as in noxious fumes; 3 syllables

∗ *resentful*: means "feelings of displeasure at some act, remark, or person"; *-ful* suffix means "full of" [resentment]; 3 syllables

∗ *insensitive*: means "lacking in feeling or tact"; prefix *-in* means "not"; 4 syllables

∗ *spiteful*: means "full of spite or malice; malicious or cruel; wishing injury, harm or suffering on another"; 2 syllables

∗ *vindictive*: means "wishing revenge on another; vengeful; showing a revengeful spirit"; 3 syllables

You may wish to have students give examples of characters in books, movies, or television who have demonstrated these emotions.

Day 2: Clustering

Ask students to arrange the 10 word cards along the top of their desk. Have students work in pairs or small groups, as discussing the words is the most important part in getting them to process the nuances of the words. Tell students to group words according to the questions below. Then allow time for pairs or groups to debate and discuss their answers.

- Which words are appropriate to use in describing the emotions or behavior of young children? Which emotions are appropriate to use in describing adults' emotions or behavior? Make two groups with your words.
- Which emotions are likely to lead to serious consequences?
- Which emotion words are similar in meaning?
- Which emotions are not likely to lead to bodily harm or injury?

Then challenge pairs or groups to arrange all the words from the mildest degree of anger and hostility to the greatest degree. Tell them to be prepared to defend their arrangements to the rest of the class.

Day 3: Word Builder

Have students separate the letters at the bottom of this week's word template. Ask them to spell words as you call them out. Call out words in the order shown below. The final word should answer the following clue: This is another word that describes a mild form of hostility or anger. (*disagreeable*)

read

readable

disable

abridge

ridge

brigade

sidebar

seabird

geese

eagles

ledge

degrees

greed

siege

seal

reseal

resealed

release

released

grease

greased

debris

desire

agile

agree

agreeable

disagreeable

As students spell each word, write it on the board. Ask them to cross-check their spelling with yours and correct any errors. Then use the list to brainstorm more words that share a spelling pattern, such as the following:

- *grease*: lease, increase, decrease, crease (-*iece* and -*eese* may make the same sound)

- *agree*: free, see (-*e* and -*y* may make the same sound)

Day 4: Word Action

To each pair or small group, give one of this week's words or allow them to choose the word. Ask them to either plan a short skit or write a short skit to demonstrate the word. Caution students not to use the word in their skits. Ask pairs or groups to read or perform their skits to see if the rest of the class can guess the word. Because several words are similar in meaning, be sure to discuss any guesses that don't match the writers' word but could possibly be acceptable.

Day 5: Word Smart

Ask students to arrange the week's words across the top of their desks with plenty of workspace below. Have them respond to your questions by picking up the correct word card(s) and holding

it so you can see the answer. If there are more than two correct answers, tell students to show only two—one in each hand. Ask: *Can you find . . .*

- a word hiding a hole in the ground? (*spiteful*)

- a word hiding a legal term for bringing a formal charge against someone? (*vindictive*)

- a word hiding something you might cover a floor with? (*hostile*)

- a word hiding a signal to go to the next class? (*belligerent*)

- a word with a part that means "harmful or injurious"?

- a word with a prefix that means "not"?

- a word that without its prefix means just the opposite?

- a word hiding a small insect? (*arrogant*)

- a word with 2 syllables?

- a word with double consonants together?

- a word with 3 syllables?

- a word hiding a word that may mean the opposite of *received*? (*resentful*)

- a word that sounds like an inexpensive hotel?

- a word that means "hardened"?

- a word that describes someone who is openly warlike and aggressive?

- a word that is a synonym for *haughty*?

- a word that means "getting back at someone"?

- a word that describes the mildest emotion of all the words?

- a word that is a metaphor for something someone might find on his or her foot?

- a word hiding a word for someone who has guests? (*hostile*)

- a word hiding something you might do to get someone's attention? (*callous*)

- a word with a suffix that means "full of "?

- a word hiding a first-person plural pronoun? (*obnoxious*)

Now ask each student to organize the words as they did in the Day 2 Clustering activity from the mildest degree of anger and hostility to the greatest degree. Have students changed their minds as they have grown more familiar with the words?

Day 1: Meet the Words

This connecting theme for this week's words is that they are all words that express degrees of sadness or negative feelings. These words are good for students to know in order state their own feelings or to use to write better descriptions. Some words differ only slightly in degree, while others show a huge difference of emotion. Don't worry about your students grasping the smallest nuances of difference. Having a general knowledge of these words will be helpful. Begin by discussing the words and whether students have heard them before and in which context.

Have students pull apart the 10 word cards for this lesson and arrange them across the top of their desks. Then ask students to do the following:

- Hold up each card as you pronounce the word on it.
- Look at the word, read it aloud, and spell it with you.
- Return the word card to the top of their desk.

Provide a definition as necessary and share some of the word's features, as described below.

* **worthless**: means "of no use or importance"; suffix -less means "without"; 2 syllables
* **forlorn**: means "dreary, unhappy, or miserable"; 2 syllables
* **lonesome**: means "lonely; sad because of a lack of companionship"; 2 syllables
* **ostracized**: means "excluded from activities, conversation, society, or communications"; sometimes means "banished from a country"; derived from the Greek word *ostreion* or *oyster* (*discuss how the word ostracized might be related to an oyster*); 3 syllables
* **alienated**: means "separated from others by feelings of hostility" ("Lars has alienated his whole family because of his attitude."); 5 syllables
* **dejected**: means "disheartened and low-spirited"; prefix de- means "away or off" (*discuss how prefix relates to the meaning of this word*); *ject* comes from the Latin word *jacere* meaning "to throw"; 3 syllables
* **depressed**: means "sad and gloomy"; base word *press* stems from the Latin word *primere*, which means "to press"; 2 syllables
* **estranged**: means "feeling a sense of separation from others"; 2 syllables
* **humiliated**: means "feeling a sense of loss of pride, self-respect or dignity"; 5 syllables

* **obsolete**: means "feeling old, no longer useful, or outmoded"; 3 syllables

You may wish to have students give examples of characters in books or movies or television who have demonstrated these emotions.

Day 2: Clustering

Ask students to arrange the 10 word cards along the top of their desk. Have students work in pairs or small groups, as discussing the words is the most important part in getting them to process the nuances of the words. Tell students to group words according to the questions below. Then allow time for pairs or groups to debate and discuss their answers.

- Which words are appropriate to use in describing the emotions and behavior of young children? Which words are appropriate to use in describing adults' emotions behavior? Which words could you use with both groups? Make three groups with your words.
- Which emotion(s) would you associate with losing a job? Tripping as you enter the classroom? Losing your best friend? Being the last to be chosen for a team? Forgetting your lines on the stage?
- Which emotion words are similar in meaning?

Then challenge pairs or groups to arrange all the words from the mildest degree of sadness (or negative feelings) to the greatest degree. Tell them to be prepared to defend their arrangements to the rest of the class.

Day 3: Word Builder

Have students separate the letters at the bottom of this week's word template. Ask them to spell words as you call them out. Call out words in the order shown below. The final word should answer the following clue: This can refer to an indentation. (*depression*)

person

disperse

dispense

preside

endorse

dense

erode

seed

speed

speeds

sore

send

sender

spend

spender

prose

spider

spine

snip

snipe

sniper

snide

snore

dispose

ripen

drone

period

redone

pressed

depress

depression

Discuss any new words and their meanings. Then, as students spell each word, write it on the board. Ask them to cross-check their spelling with yours and correct any errors. Then use the list to brainstorm more words that share a spelling pattern, such as the following:

- *spend*: bend, tend, send, extend, intend, stipend

- *depress*: express, impress, process, dress, bless

Day 4: Word Action

To each pair or small group, give one of this week's words or allow them to choose the word. Ask them to write a short skit to demonstrate the word. Caution students not to use the word in their skits. Ask pairs or groups to read or perform their skits to see if the rest of the class can guess the word. Because several words are similar in meaning, be sure to discuss any incorrect guesses that could possibly be acceptable.

Day 5: Word Smart

Ask students to arrange the week's words across the top of their desks with plenty of workspace below. Have them respond to your questions by picking up the correct word card(s) and holding it so you can see the answer. If there are more than two correct answers, tell students to show only two—one in each hand. Ask: *Can you find . . .*

- a word hiding a number? (*lonesome*)

- a word that describes the feeling that one could easily be replaced?

- a word that indicates that someone is being separated from others?

- a word that originated with an oyster?

- a word hiding a part of the foot? (*obsolete*)

- a word that starts with a prefix?

- a word hiding a way to sing a song without using words?

- a word with a suffix that means "without"?

- a word that starts with a vowel?

- a word hiding a word that completes this song title: "Home on the _____."? (*estranged*)

- a word with 5 syllables?

- a word that has 2 o's?

- a word hiding a being from another planet? (*alienated*)

- a word hiding a word that means a small amount? (*lonesome*)

- a word hiding a synonym for *push*? (*depressed*)

- a word with the same ending as *athlete*?

- a word that means "sad because of a lack of friends or companions"?

- a word hiding a homophone for a number? (*forlorn*)

Now ask students to organize the words as they did in the Day 2 Clustering activity from the mildest degree of depression to the greatest degree. Have students changed their minds as they have grown more familiar with the words?

Day 1: Meet the Words

This week's words are split between high-frequency words and emotion/quality words. Several words express the quality of caring. Some words differ only slightly in degree, while others show a huge difference of emotion. Don't worry about your students' grasping the smallest nuances of difference. Having a general knowledge of these words will be helpful. Begin by discussing the words and whether students have heard them before and in which context.

Have students pull apart the 10 word cards for this lesson and arrange them across the top of their desks. Then ask students to do the following:

- Hold up each card as you pronounce the word on it.
- Look at the word, read it aloud, and spell it with you.
- Return the word card to the top of their desk.

Provide a definition as necessary and share some of the word's features, as described below.

* **suddenly**: high-frequency word; -ly ending signals that it's an adverb; means "quickly"; 3 syllables

* **direction**: high-frequency word; noun with multiple meanings: 1) "act of directing" ("We need you to offer us some direction to get the play organized."); 2) "a point or region" ("The direction we are traveling in is north."); 3) "a line along which something moves" ("The storm is moving in a southerly direction."); 4) "a purpose or goal" ("Kate doesn't seem to have any direction in her life."); -ion suffix signals a noun; 3 syllables

* **anything**: high-frequency word; compound word: any + thing; 2 syllables

* **divided**: high-frequency word; means "separated"; 3 syllables

* **general**: high-frequency word; adjective usage ("pertaining to all people or things"; also can mean "non-specific") and noun ("military officer"); 3 syllables

* **amiable**: describes a personal quality that is pleasant, good-natured, and friendly; 4 syllables

* **altruistic**: describes a personal quality that demonstrates unselfish concern for the welfare of others; -ic suffix forms an adjective meaning "characteristic of"; 4 syllables

* **charitable**: describes a quality of kindness and generosity toward relieving the burdens of others"; -able suffix changes noun charity into an adjective meaning "capable of" charity; 4 syllables

* **empathetic**: describes someone who can experience the feelings, thoughts, and attitudes of another person (explore the difference between sympathetic and empathetic: sympathy is feeling sorrow for someone, whereas empathy

is feeling sorrow with that person—actually knowing how they are feeling); related to empathy and empathize; -ic suffix changes noun into an adjective meaning "characteristic of"; 4 syllables

* **humane**: means "the quality of someone who is tender and compassionate toward other people and/or animals"; many towns and cities have a humane society (discuss how this word relates to the mission of these societies); (explore how the word humane relates to the base word human); 2 syllables

You may wish to have students give examples of characters in books or movies or television who have demonstrated the 5 emotion words.

Day 2: Clustering

Ask students to arrange the 5 word cards that identify qualities of caring along the top of their desk. Have students work in pairs or small groups, as discussing the words is the most important part in getting them to process the nuances of the words. Tell students to group words according to the questions below. Then allow time for pairs or groups to debate and discuss their answers.

- Which qualities are most likely to be directed toward people? Which are mostly likely to be directed toward animals? Which words could you use with both groups? Make three groups with your word cards.

- Which of these qualities might involve monetary donations? Which qualities involve other types of contributions (time, energy)?

- Which qualities are similar in meaning?

- What other words can students list that are used to describe other caring quality words?

Then challenge pairs or groups to arrange all the words from the mildest degree of caring to the greatest degree. Tell them to be prepared to defend their arrangements to the rest of the class.

Day 3: Word Builder

Have students separate the letters at the bottom of this week's word template. Ask them to spell words as you call them out. Call out words in the order shown below. The final word should answer the following clue: We should all strive to display this quality. (charitable)

earth
later

alert

latch

trail

trial

brace

batch

rehab

beach

bleach

trial

caliber

article

recital

ethical

herbal

table

chair

chart

heart

charitable

Discuss any new words and their meanings. As students spell each word, write it on the board. Ask them to cross-check their spelling with yours and correct any errors. Then use the list to brainstorm more words that share a spelling pattern, such as the following:

- *latch*: batch, match, hatch, mismatch, snatch, dispatch
- *trail*: entail, mail, jail, shirttail, derail (-*ale* makes the same sound)

Day 4: Word Action

To each pair or small group, give one of this week's words or allow them to choose the word. Ask them to write a short skit to demonstrate the word. Caution students not to use the word in their skits. Ask pairs or groups to read or perform their skits to see if the rest of the class can guess the word. Because several words are similar in meaning, be sure to discuss any incorrect guesses that could possibly be acceptable.

Day 5: Word Smart

Ask students to arrange the week's words across the top of their desks

with plenty of workspace below. Have them respond to your questions by picking up the correct word card(s) and holding it so you can see the answer. If there are more than two correct answers, tell students to show only two—one in each hand. Ask: *Can you find . . .*

- a word that is a compound?
- a word hiding a route through the woods? (*emp*athetic)
- a word that may mean "broad"?
- a word that has a suffix that signals that it is an adverb?
- a word hiding what we all are? (*human*e)
- a word that can name a person in the military?
- a word that means "separated"?
- a word that describes someone who can relate to the sadness or emotional state of another?
- a word that describes people who give selflessly to help others?
- a word that describes someone who is compassionate and kind to other people and/or animals?
- a word that describes someone who is friendly?
- a word that can be a synonym for *quickly*?
- a word hiding the home of a bear? (*sud*den*ly*)
- a word that has 4 syllables?
- a word with 2 syllables?
- a word that describes north, south, east, or west?
- a word hiding a word that means "straight to the point"? (*direct*ion)
- a word that means "non-specific"?
- a word that has 2 letters at the beginning that together say a letter name?

Now ask students to return the words to the top of their desks. Their next challenge is to sort the words by a common characteristic. Then have partners share their work by asking each other, "What's my rule?" The guesses may include valid categories, but the correct answer is the partner's rule. Here are some sample categories for this week's words:

- *suddenly, direction, anything, divided, general* (words with 3 syllables)
- *anything, amiable, altruistic, empathetic* (words that start with a vowel)
- *direction, divided, altruistic* (words with 2 *i*'s)
- *altruistic, charitable* (qualities that require more than compassion—generosity of some kind)

Day 1: Meet the Words

This week's words are split between high-frequency words and words that express joy. These words are good for students to know in order state their own feelings or to use to write better descriptions. Some words differ only slightly in degree, while others show a huge difference in emotion. Don't worry about your students grasping the smallest nuances of difference. Having a general knowledge of these words will be helpful. Begin by discussing the words and whether students have heard them before and in which context.

Have students pull apart the 10 word cards for this lesson and arrange them across the top of their desks. Then ask students to do the following:

- Hold up each card as you pronounce the word on it.
- Look at the word, read it aloud, and spell it with you.
- Return the word card to the top of their desk.

Provide a definition as necessary and share some of the word's features, as described below.

- ✳ *energy*: high-frequency word; also used often in science; multiple meanings: 1) the capacity or power to do work ("Fossil fuel, the sun, and electricity are sources of energy."), 2) the capacity for vigorous activity ("Eating a healthy lunch will give me the energy to work out this afternoon.")
- ✳ *subject*: high-frequency word; heteronym (words that are spelled alike but have different origins and pronunciations): with stress on first syllable, has meanings that are nouns and adjectives, one of which is a course of study at school; with stress on second syllable, is a verb that means "to cause to undergo an experience" ("We were subjected to the noise of the alarm for an hour."); 2 syllables
- ✳ *region*: high-frequency word; a noun that means "a specified area"; 2 syllables
- ✳ *believe*: high-frequency word; often misspelled: remember that there is an *e* on either side of the *v*; 2 syllables
- ✳ *exercise*: high-frequency word; noun usage ("Walking is good exercise.") and verb usage ("We will exercise after school."); frequently misspelled: *exer* not *excer*; 3 syllables
- ✳ *ecstatic*: means "experiencing great joy or ecstasy"; 3 syllables
- ✳ *enthusiastic*: means "in a state of emotion of excitement or enthusiasm"; 5 syllables
- ✳ *elated*: means "experiencing extreme pride or happiness"; 3 syllables

- ✳ *gratified*: means "feeling of satisfaction"; 3 syllables
- ✳ *vivacious*: means "displaying liveliness or animation"; 3 syllables

You may wish to have students give examples of characters in books or movies or television who have demonstrated joyous emotion.

Day 2: Clustering

Ask students to arrange the 5 word cards that express joy along the top of their desks. Have students work in pairs or small groups, as discussing the words is the most important part in getting them to process the nuances of the words. Tell students to group words according to the questions below. Then allow time for pairs or groups to debate and discuss their answers.

- Which words refer to emotional states that are the most similar?
- Which qualities are part of someone's personality and which are related to outside circumstances?
- What circumstances at school might evoke these different emotions?
- What other words can you think of that describe levels of joy? Where do they fall in the range from least joyful to most joyful?

Then challenge pairs or groups to arrange all the words from the mildest degree of joy to the greatest degree. Tell them to be prepared to defend their arrangements to the rest of the class. Finally, ask students to think of other words that describe levels of joy and to rank them from the mildest to the greatest degree of that emotion.

Day 3: Word Builder

Have students separate the letters at the bottom of this week's word template. Ask them to spell words as you call them out. Call out words in the order shown below. The final word should answer the following clue: This could describe a fan watching her favorite team play. (*enthusiastic*)

nice

nicest

suitcase

authentic

situate

chase

insist

intact

ethic

ethnic

snitch

snatch

shiniest

sinus

sauce

cause

acute

chain

issue

tissue

static

staunch

sustain

enthusiastic

Discuss any new words and their meanings. As students spell each word, write it on the board. Ask them to cross-check their spelling with yours and correct any errors. Then use the list to brainstorm more words that share a spelling pattern, such as the following:

- *insist*: enlist, resist, persist, consist, assist

- *sustain*: retain, abstain, detain, train, chain

Day 4: Word Action

To each pair or small group, give one of this week's words or allow them to choose the word. Ask them to write a short skit to demonstrate the word. Caution students not to use the word in their skits. Ask pairs or groups to read or perform their skits to see if the rest of the class can guess the word. Because several words are similar in meaning, be sure to discuss any incorrect guesses that could possibly be acceptable.

Day 5: Word Smart

Ask students to arrange the week's words across the top of their desks with plenty of workspace below. Have them respond to your questions by picking up the correct word card(s) and holding it so you can see the answer. If there are more than two correct answers, tell students to show only two—one in each hand. Ask: *Can you find . . .*

- a word that has 5 syllables?

- a word that can be pronounced two different ways, depending upon how it's used?

- a word that refers to a specific area?

- a word that is always a verb?

- a word hiding a type of electricity? (*ec**static***)

- a word hiding the opposite of *early*? (*el**ated***)

- a word hiding a rodent? (*g**rat**ified*)

- a word hiding a pronoun other than *I*? (*vivacio**us***)

- a word that means "satisfied or fulfilled"?

- a word that means "lively"?

- a word connected to the noun *ecstasy*?

- a word represented by walking, running, yoga, and swimming?

- a word represented by sun, wind, and electricity?

- a word hiding a slang word for a type of large sandwich?

- a word with 2 long-vowel sounds?

- a word with an /er/ sound?

- a word that, if you changed the first letter to *r*, would mean "to ease"?

Now ask students to return the words to the top of their desks. Their next challenge is to sort the words by a common characteristic. Then have partners share their work by asking each other, "What's my rule?" The guesses may include valid categories, but the correct answer is the partner's rule. Here are some sample categories for this week's words:

- *ecstatic, enthusiastic, elated, gratified, vivacious* (feelings of joy)

- *energy, exercise* (you need to use one to accomplish the other)

- *subject, region, believe* (2 syllables)

- *believe, exercise* (verbs)

Day 1: Meet the Words

This week's words are split between high-frequency and commonly misspelled words and words that are associated with governments. Having a general knowledge of these words will be helpful. Begin by discussing the words and whether students have heard them before and in which context.

Have students pull apart the 12 word cards for this lesson and arrange them across the top of their desks. Then ask students to do the following:

- Hold up each card as you pronounce the word on it.
- Look at the word, read it aloud, and spell it with you.
- Return the word card to the top of their desk.

Provide a definition as necessary and share some of the word's features, as described below.

* **developed**: high-frequency word; verb usage (past tense of *develop*—no e at the end!) meaning "grown or brought to a more advanced state", and adjective usage ("The United States is a developed nation."); 3 syllables
* **difference**: high-frequency word; means "inconsistency or inequality"; tricky spelling with 2 f's and -ence (not -ance!) ending; 3 syllables
* **probably**: high-frequency word; adverb ending -ly; means "very likely"; related to *probable* and *probability*; 3 syllables
* **written**: high-frequency word; remember the 2 t's; 2 syllables
* **length**: high-frequency word; also used often in math for measurement (the length of a board); tricky spelling because of g
* **dictatorship**: means "government ruled by one unelected leader (dictator) without hereditary succession who forces or coerces people into following"; originated with the Latin word *dictator,* who was a judge who had absolute power; 4 syllables

Note: In the rest of the words, the word part *cracy* means "power."

* **monarchy**: means "government ruled by a king or queen whose leadership is passed down the family line"; sometimes refers to a constitutional monarchy in which rule is also based on a country's constitution; word part *mon* is related to *mono*, which means "one" plus *archy*, which means "rule"; 3 syllables
* **anarchy**: means "a chaotic state without government, perhaps where a ruler has been overthrown"; word part *an* means "without" plus *archy*, which means "rule"; 3 syllables

* **aristocracy**: means "government ruled by a group of the upper class and elite (aristocrats)"; derived from the Greek word meaning "ruled by the best"; word part *aristos* means "best"; 5 syllables
* **autocracy**: means "government whose ruler who has unlimited authority"; from the Greek word *auto* meaning "self" (autobiography, automobile); 4 syllables
* **democracy**: means "government by the people"; the United States has a presidential democracy; the United Kingdom has a parliamentary democracy; Greek word *demos* means "common people"; 4 syllables
* **theocracy**: means "form of government in which a god or deity is acknowledged as the holder of supreme power and religious laws are interpreted by authorities"; Greek word *theos* means "god"; related to *theology*, which is the study of religious truth; 4 syllables

Day 2: Clustering

Ask students to arrange the 7 word cards that are associated with government along the top of their desk. Have students work in pairs or small groups, as discussing the words is the most important part in getting them to process the nuances of the words. Tell students to group words according to the questions below. Then allow time for pairs or groups to debate and discuss their answers.

- Which governmental system seems tolerable and which seems intolerable to you? Make 2 stacks of word cards and be prepared to defend your decision.
- Arrange the 7 words in order from the most to the least effective governmental systems. Defend your decision.
- Arrange your 7 words in order from the most to the least efficient governmental systems. Defend your decision.
- Arrange your 7 words in order from the most to the least fair governmental systems. Defend your decision.

Day 3: Word Builder

Have students separate the letters at the bottom of this week's word template. Ask them to spell words as you call them out. Call out words in the order shown below. The final word should answer the following clue: The leader of this type of government can't be voted out of office. (*dictatorship*)

taco

third

thirst

sport

shirt

chair

poach

roach

chaos

tacit

captor

actor

coats

coast

hoist

dispatch

drastic

rap

scrap

spirit

script

stitch

ship

topics

tropic

postcard

dictator

dictatorship

Discuss any new words and their meanings. As students spell each word, write it on the board. Ask them to cross-check their spelling with yours and correct any errors. Then use the list to brainstorm more words that share a spelling pattern, such as the following:

- *ship*; dip, flip, filmstrip, hardship, parsnip, chip
- *tropic*: clinic, chronic, caustic, attic, cosmic, drastic (*-ick* makes the same sound)

Day 4: Choices

Option 1: Have partners or small groups use the 7 words associated with government to brainstorm what they consider to be the pros and cons of each of the systems. Even if students find the system to be intolerant, have them find at least one pro statement for each system.

Option 2: **Word Action:** To each pair or small group, give one of the 7 governmental words or allow them to choose the word. Ask them to write a short skit to demonstrate the word. Caution students not to use the word in their skits. Ask pairs or groups to read or perform their skits to see if the rest of the class can guess the word. Because several words are similar in meaning, be sure to discuss any incorrect guesses that might be acceptable.

Day 5: Word Smart

Ask students to arrange the week's words across the top of their desks with plenty of workspace below. Have them respond to your questions by picking up the correct word card(s) and holding it so you can see the answer. If there are more than two correct answers, tell students to show only two—one in each hand. Ask: *Can you find . . .*

- a word that is in the past tense?
- a word that has a word part that means "self"?
- a word hiding a mode of transportation? (*dictatorship*)
- a word part that comes from the word for "best" in Greek?
- a word part that means "god" in Greek?
- a word that means "the longest dimension of something"?
- a word that means the opposite of *unlikely*?
- a word that means the opposite of *similarity*?
- a word that has double consonants?
- a word with a word part that means "common people" in Greek?
- a word that describes the form of government that has hereditary rulers?
- a word with a word part that means "one"?
- a word that is an adjective that might be used to describe a country?
- a word that is a synonym for *inequality*?
- a word that describes a system ruled by kings and queens?
- a word that describes a government based on religious laws and principles?
- a word that means "a lack of government and rule"?
- a word that relates to the upper class and the elite?

Now ask students to return the words to the top of their desks. Their next challenge is to sort the words by a common characteristic. Then have partners share their work by asking each other, "What's my rule?" The guesses may include valid categories, but the correct answer is the partner's rule. Here are some sample categories for this week's words:

- *difference, written* (words with double consonants)
- *aristocracy, autocracy, dictatorship, monarchy, theocracy* (systems where the common person has no voice)
- *aristocracy, autocracy, democracy, theocracy* (words that have a word part that means "power")

Day 1: Meet the Words

This week's vocabulary is made up of high-frequency words and vivid verbs that can be used effectively in writing to replace the overused word *said*.

Have students pull apart the 12 word cards for this lesson and arrange them across the top of their desks. Then ask students to do the following:

- Hold up each card as you pronounce the word on it.
- Look at the word, read it aloud, and spell it with you.
- Return the word card to the top of their desk.

Provide a definition as necessary and share some of the word's features, as described below.

* **reason**: high-frequency word; noun usage has multiple meanings, among them "basis or cause for some belief" or "good sense"; verb usage means "to think in a logical manner"; tricky *ea* combination with long-*e* sound; 2 syllables

* **present**: high-frequency word; heteronym (words that are spelled alike but have different meanings and pronunciations); when first syllable is stressed, has multiple meanings: "a gift," "in attendance," or "the current time period"; when second syllable is stressed, means "to bring, offer, or show," as in "Let me present our guest."

* **beautiful**: high-frequency word; usually used in adjective form to mean "very pleasing to hear, see, or think about"; suffix -*ful* added to base word *beauty*; 3 syllables

* **edge**: high-frequency word; tricky spelling because *d* is not enunciated; comes from the Greek word *ecke*, meaning "corner"; idiom: "Set one's teeth on edge."

* **sign**: high-frequency word; multiple meanings of verb and noun usage from "hint or suggestion" to "to communicate with a language of hand signals"; related to *signal* and *signage*; tricky spelling because of silent *g*

* **asserted**: means "stated with confidence," as in "'I will take my luggage now!' Lou asserted."; past tense of *assert*; 3 syllables

* **cautioned**: means "warned or alerted," as in "'They could be coming at any time,' my mother cautioned."; past tense of *caution*; 2 syllables

* **bellowed**: means "roared," as in "'I am leaving right now!' bellowed the farmer."; past tense of *bellow*; word originated as a reference to noisy animals; 2 syllables

* **interrupted**: means "broke into conversation to interject something," as in "'Let me handle that,' she interrupted."; related to *interrupt* and *rupture*; prefix *inter-* means "between"; 4 syllables

* **responded**: means "replied or answered," as in "'Yes, I want to go,' Mrs. Lomax responded immediately."; past tense of *respond*; 3 syllables

* **taunted**: means "teased or mocked," as in "'You are not the champion you claim to be!' the boy taunted."; tricky spelling with *au* combination—notice the word *aunt* embedded; past tense of *taunt*; 2 syllables

* **demanded**: means "asked urgently with authority," as in "'I want you to leave immediately!' the judge demanded."; past tense of *demand*; related to *mandate*; 3 syllables

Day 2: Clustering

Ask students to arrange the 7 word cards that are synonyms for *said* along the top of their desk. Have students work in pairs or small groups, as discussing the words is the most important part in getting them to process the nuances of the words. Tell students to group words according to the questions below. Then allow time for pairs or groups to debate and discuss their answers.

- Arrange the 7 words in the order of the most polite to the least polite way of replacing the word *said*. Defend your choices.

- Which words would most likely be used to describe a child's dialogue? Which words would you use to describe an adult's dialogue? Which words would you use for both? Make 3 groups of words.

Day 3: Word Builder

Have students separate the letters at the bottom of this week's word template. Ask them to spell words as you call them out. Call out words in the order shown below. The final word should answer the following clue: A whine that can replace the word *said*. (*complained*)

model	impend	calm
panic	implode	calmed
manic	impaled	candle
denial	clamped	camel
dance	cinema	compile
omen	anemic	compel
poem	pandemic	complain
place	police	complained
demonic	pencil	

Discuss any new words and their meanings. As students spell each word, write it on the board. Ask them to cross-check their spelling with yours and correct any errors. Then use the list to brainstorm more words that share a spelling pattern, such as the following:

- *dance*: France, chance, finance, entrance, enhance, prance
- *place*: grace, face, embrace, disgrace, trace, shoelace

Day 4: Comics or Word Action

Option 1: **Comics:** Go to a search engine and find comic strip templates to copy for your students. Have students work individually, with partners, or in small groups to create a comic strip script with dialogue that uses many or all of the 7 words in place of *said*. Then have them draw the comics. Encourage them to share their creations. Be sure to comment on word choices that relate well to the situation shown in the comic strip.

Option 2: **Word Action:** To each pair or small group, give one of the 7 words or allow them to choose the word. Ask them to write a short skit to demonstrate the word. Caution students not to use the word in their skits. Ask pairs or groups to read or perform their skits to see if the rest of the class can guess the word. Because several words are similar in meaning, be sure to discuss any incorrect guesses that could possibly be acceptable.

Day 5: Word Smart

Ask students to arrange the week's words across the top of their desks with plenty of workspace below. Have them respond to your questions by picking up the correct word card(s) and holding it so you can see the answer. If there are more than two correct answers, tell students to show only two—one in each hand. Ask: *Can you find . . .*

- a word that may be a gift?
- a word with a long-*i* sound?
- a word with a silent *d*?
- a word hiding a male child? (*rea**son***)
- a word hiding an adult male? (*de**man**ded*)
- a word hiding something you can ring? (*be**ll**owed*)
- a word with a silent *g*?
- a word hiding a small body of water? (*res**pond**ed*)
- a word hiding an antonym for *down*? (*inter**rup**ted*)
- a word hiding the sister to one of your parents? (*t**aunt**ed*)
- a word hiding the opposite of *high*? (*be**llow**ed*)
- a word that might be represented by *stop*, *yield*, *curve*, or *65*?
- a word that could mean "butted in"?
- a word that means "mocked or provoked"?
- a word that means "stated with confidence"?
- a word that might be used to describe sunsets, people, a beach, or the mountains?
- a word that tells what you might need if you're late to class?
- a word that means "to introduce"?
- a word that is sometimes used with "cutting," "living on," or "of a cliff"?
- a word that means "replied or answered"?
- a word that means "warned or alerted"?
- a word that means "ordered with authority"?
- a word that means "hollered"?
- a word with a prefix that means "between"?

Now ask students to return the words to the top of their desks. Their next challenge is to sort the words by a common characteristic. Then have partners share their work by asking each other, "What's my rule?" The guesses may include valid categories, but the correct answer is the partner's rule. Here are some sample categories for this week's words:

- *asserted, cautioned, bellowed, interrupted, responded, taunted, demanded* (past-tense verbs)
- *asserted, bellowed, interrupted* (words with double consonants)
- *beautiful, asserted, cautioned, edge, demanded* (words that begin with one of the first five letters of the alphabet)
- *present, taunted, demanded* (words that end with the first letter of the next word in the series)

Day 1: Meet the Words

This week's vocabulary is made up of high-frequency words and words that end in -ism that will be useful for students to know.

Have students pull apart the 12 word cards for this lesson and arrange them across the top of their desks. Then ask students to do the following:

- Hold up each card as you pronounce the word on it.
- Look at the word, read it aloud, and spell it with you.
- Return the word card to the top of their desk.

Provide a definition as necessary and share some of the word's features, as described below.

* **finished**: high-frequency word; past-tense verb meaning "ended or completed"; 2 syllables

* **discovered**: high-frequency word; past tense verb meaning "found or took notice of"; difference between *invented* and *discovered*: *invent* is "to create"; *discover* refers to something that already exists; prefix *dis-* means "the opposite of," as in "the opposite of covered up"; 3 syllables

* **beside**: high-frequency word; used often as a preposition ("beside the road"); *Note*: for the preposition that means "over" and "above", *besides* is preferred as in, "Ally earned this honor for doing something besides her normal duties."; 2 syllables

* **million**: high-frequency word often misspelled; tricky spelling with double *l* and the *ion* combination; cardinal number; 2 syllables

* **lie**: high-frequency word; has two different origins and multiple meanings: 1) a noun meaning "an untruth," or a verb meaning "to tell something untrue", or 2) a verb, which means "to recline" (*lie, lay, lain*); idioms for both words: "lying through your teeth" and "lying down on the job"

* **perhaps**: high-frequency word; adverb meaning "possibly" or "maybe"; 2 syllables

Note: Each of the following words contain the suffix *-ism*, which means "principle, policy, or doctrine"

* **imperialism**: means "a policy of extending governmental rule into foreign lands"; 6 syllables

* **fascism**: means "a political movement or philosophy in which a dictator controls all commerce and industry and opposes democracy"; tricky pronunciation and spelling because of *sc*; 3 syllables

* **communism**: means "a system of social organization in which all property is held in common, with the goal of a classless society"; 4 syllables

* **patriotism**: means "devoted love and support of one's country"; 5 syllables

* **capitalism**: means "an economic system in which wealth is made and maintained by private individuals"; related to *capital*, which means "wealth or profit"; 5 syllables

* **socialism**: means "a system of social organization that invests a portion of its wealth in the community"; 4 syllables

Day 2: Picture That

Ask students to find and arrange the 6 -ism words across the top of their desks. Next, have them fold a sheet of paper lengthwise (hot-dog style) and then fold it into thirds to create 6 equal boxes. As you review the definitions and discuss each of the words that end in -ism, students write the word in one of the boxes. After the discussion, tell them to sketch a picture that will help them remember the meaning of each word.

Day 3: Word Builder

Have students separate the letters at the bottom of this week's word template. Ask them to spell words as you call them out. Call out words in the order shown below. The final word should answer the following clue: This is an -ism that most of us experience. (*patriotism*)

omit

impair

import

moist

trim

port

sport

stomp

storm

stamp

strap

smart

soap

trait

riot

roam

pastor

roast

toast

trio

spirit

patriot

patriotism

Discuss any new words and their meanings. As students spell each word, write it on the board. Ask them to cross-check their spelling with yours and correct any errors. Then use the list to brainstorm more words that share a spelling pattern, such as the following:

- *impair*: air, fair, hair, chair, affair (-*are* and -*ear* make the same sound)

- *port*: support, deport, export, sort, transport (-*art* makes the same sound: *wart, quart, depart*)

Day 4: Linkage

Tell students to see how many words they can find in the chain of letters on the Linkage Word Strips reproducible (page 127). The chain includes weekly words, as well as other words. See who can find the most words and discuss the words that students think are interesting. You might ask students to write on the board the most unusual word they found.

Day 5: Word Smart

Ask students to arrange the week's words across the top of their desks with plenty of workspace below. Have them respond to your questions by picking up the correct word card(s) and

holding it so you can see the answer. If there are more than two correct answers, tell students to show only two—one in each hand. Ask: *Can you find . . .*

- a word hiding a body part of a fish? (*fin*ished)

- a word hiding a factory where people work? (*mill*ion)

- a word hiding a word that means "to conceal or hide"? (dis*cover*ed)

- a word hiding something you might wear to a ball game? (ca*pit*alism)

- a word for "telling a fib"?

- a word hiding a person who loves his or her country? (*patriot*ism)

- a word hiding a place to store tools? (fini*shed*)

- a word for a system in which money is made and kept by individuals and corporations?

- a word for a government policy whose goal is the territorial growth of the country?

- a word that is represented by a number with 7 digits?

- a word that means "found or learned about something"?

- a word that is a preposition?

- a word that is an adverb?

- a word for a system that would allow a citizen to work hard and become a millionaire?

- a word for a system that would not allow a citizen to work hard and become a millionaire?

- a word hiding a pronoun besides *I*? (fin*ishe*d)

- a word with a prefix that means "the opposite of"?

- a word that means "to recline"?

- a word that means "the love of and support for one's country"?

- a word with a suffix that means "a principle, policy or doctrine"?

- a word hiding a word that means "three people acting together"? (pa*trio*tism)

- a word that is a system where a dictator controls all the commerce and wealth?

Day 1: Meet the Words

This week's vocabulary is made up of high-frequency words and words that describe phobias. Having a general knowledge of these words will be helpful. Begin by discussing the words and whether students have heard them before and in which context.

Have students pull apart the 12 word cards for this lesson and arrange them across the top of their desks. Then ask students to do the following:

- Hold up each card as you pronounce the word on it.
- Look at the word, read it aloud, and spell it with you.
- Return the word card to the top of their desk.

Provide a definition as necessary and share some of the word's features, as described below.

* **weather**: high-frequency word; frequently misspelled and also confused with *whether*; tricky *ea* vowel combination; 2 syllables

* **instruments**: high-frequency word; frequently misspelled; can refer to musical or mechanical tools; 3 syllables

* **third**: high-frequency word; ordinal number after *second* and before *fourth*; *ir* sound is also made by *er* and *ur* in other words

* **include**: high-frequency word; verb usage; 2 syllables

* **built**: high-frequency word; past tense of *build*

* **glossary**: means "the alphabetical listing of terms with definitions that appear in the back of books"; originated from both Latin and Greek words: Greek *glossa* originally meant "tongue," was next defined as "word," and eventually became "to explain a word or text"; the Latin word *glossa* was a word that needed explanation

Note: Each of the following words contains the word part *phobia*, which means "fear."

* **aquaphobia**: means "fear of water"; Latin word part *aqua-* means "water" as in, *aquamarine* and *aquarium*; 5 syllables

* **hemophobia**: means "fear of blood"; *hemo* means "blood" as in, *hemoglobin* and *hemophilia*; 5 syllables

* **claustrophobia**: means "fear of enclosed spaces"; *claustro* comes from the Latin word meaning "cloister or enclosed space"; 5 syllables

* **astraphobia**: means "fear of thunder and lightning"; *ast* is the Greek word for "star" as in, *astronaut* and *astra* means "lightning"; 5 syllables

* **optophobia**: means "fear of opening one's eyes"; *opto* means "optic or vision" as in, *optical* and *optic nerve*; 5 syllables

* **amaxophobia**: means "fear of riding in or driving a vehicle"; *amaxa* is the Greek word for "carriage"; 6 syllables

Day 2: Picture That

Ask students to find and arrange the 6 -*phobia* words across the top of their desks. Next, have them fold a sheet of paper lengthwise (hot-dog style) and then fold it into thirds to create 6 equal boxes. As you review the definitions and discuss each of the words that end in -*phobia*, students write the word in one of the boxes. After the discussion, tell them to sketch a picture that will help them remember the meaning of each word. You might add *arachibutyrophobia*—the fear that peanut butter will stick to the roof of your mouth—or have students create a phobia to name and sketch.

Day 3: Word Builder

Have students separate the letters at the bottom of this week's word template. Ask them to spell words as you call them out. Call out words in the order shown below. The final word should answer the following clue: This fear of eight-legged creatures is a fairly common phobia! (*arachnophobia*)

rain

pain

brain

chain

hair

choir

anchor

orphan

piano

pinch

honor

rhino

roach

broach

ranch

branch

arch

parch

porch

poncho

honcho

carbon

phobia

arachnophobia

Discuss any new words and their meanings. As students spell each word, write it on the board. Ask them to cross-check their spelling with yours and correct any errors. Then use the list to brainstorm more words that share a spelling pattern, such as the following:

- *brain*: gain, drain, Spain, chain, stain, detain
- *roach*: coach, approach, reproach

Day 4: Linkage

Tell students to see how many words they can find in the chain of letters on the Linkage Word Strips reproducible (page 127). The chain includes weekly words, as well as other words. See who can find the most words and discuss the words that students think are interesting. You might ask students to write on the board the most unusual word they found.

Day 5: Word Smart

Ask students to arrange the week's words across the top of their desks with plenty of workspace below. Have them respond to your questions by picking up the correct word card(s) and holding it so you can see the answer. If there are more than two correct answers, tell students to show only two—one in each hand. Ask: *Can you find . . .*

- a word that has a word part that means "water"?

- a word that is a plural?

- a word that has a word part that means "blood"?

- a word that grew from the word "tongue"?

- a word hiding pronouns besides *I*? (*weather, instruments*)

- a word with a word part that means "fear"?

- a word with a word part that means "vehicle or carriage"?

- a word with a word part that means "lightning"?

- a word that is an ordinal number?

- a word that is in the past tense?

- a word represented by "rain," "sleet," "snow," "sunny"?

- a word that names part of a book?

- a word hiding something you do at mealtime? (*weather*)

- a word with a word part that means "cloister or enclosed space"?

- a word with a word part that means "vision"?

- a word with a part that means "star"?

- a word hiding something that is at the apex or highest point? (*amaxophobia*)

- a word that comes after *second*?

- a word that is an antonym for *exclude*?

Have students arrange the words for phobias in order of those that they think are experienced by the greatest to the least number of people. Compare their results and have fun discussing them!

Day 1: Meet the Words

This week's vocabulary is made up of high-frequency words and words with the -ology suffix. Having a general knowledge of these words will be helpful. Begin by discussing the words and whether students have heard them before and in which context.

Have students pull apart the 12 word cards for this lesson and arrange them across the top of their desks. Then ask students to do the following:

- Hold up each card as you pronounce the word on it.
- Look at the word, read it aloud, and spell it with you.
- Return the word card to the top of their desk.

Provide a definition as necessary and share some of the word's features, as described below.

* **represent**: high-frequency word; verb meaning "to stand for or to act on behalf of;" 3 syllables

* **whether**: high-frequency word and frequently misspelled; distinguished from *weather* by the beginning /hw/ sound; common use as a conjunction; 2 syllables

* **clothes**: high-frequency word; similar pronunciation as the word *close*; related to *cloth* and *clothe*

* **flowers**: high-frequency word; plural; sounds similar to the word *flour*; 2 syllables

* **teacher**: high-frequency word; -er suffix means "one who" [teaches]; tricky spelling with *ea* combination making long-e sound; 2 syllables

* **couldn't**: high-frequency word; contraction for *could not*; apostrophe used for omitted letter *o*; contraction used in everyday, informal speech

Note: Each of the following words contains the suffix -ology, which means "the study of."

* **anthropology**: means "the study of people or mankind"; originated with the Greek word *anthropos*, which means "human"; a person who studies is an anthropologist, with the -ist meaning "person"; 5 syllables

* **cardiology**: means "the study of the heart"; *cardio-* means "heart"; a cardiologist is a heart specialist; 5 syllables

* **ethnology**: means "a branch of anthropology that studies the historical development of cultures and races"; *ethno* comes from the Greek word *ethnos*, which means "race"; an ethnologist is a specialist in this science; 4 syllables

* **dermatology** means "the study of the skin"; *derma* comes from a Greek word for "skin or hide"; a dermatologist is a skin specialist; 5 syllables

* **meteorology**: means "the study of the atmosphere—weather and climate"; *meteor* comes from a Greek word meaning "something aloft"; 6 syllables

* **psychology**: means "the study of the mind"; *psych* comes from the Greek word *psyche*, which means "spirit or soul"; related to *psychiatry, psychological, psychologist, psychopath*, which all deal with the mind and human behavior; 4 syllables

Day 2: Picture That

Ask students to find and arrange the 6 ology words across the top of their desks. Next, have them fold a sheet of paper lengthwise (hot-dog style) and then fold it into thirds to create 6 equal boxes. As you review the definitions and discuss each of the words that end in ology, students write the word in one of the boxes. After the discussion, tell them to sketch a picture that will help them remember the meaning of each word. You might also ask students to create a new ology to name and sketch. Have fun sharing these!

Day 3: Word Builder

Have students separate the letters at the bottom of this week's word template. Ask them to spell words as you call them out. Call out words in the order shown below. The final word should answer the following clue: This person has his or her heart in what he or she does. (cardiologist)

said

girls

drastic

tragic

solicit

solicitor

adroit

discolor

digits

logic

logistic

cordial

 Systematic Word Study for Grades 4–6 © 2011 by Cheryl M. Sigmon • Scholastic Teaching Resources • Lesson 24

acrid

garlic

solid

stood

cargo

idol

social

aortic

locator

rigid

igloo

tidal

radio

gratis

cardiologist

Discuss any new words and their meanings. Share that one of the words, *aortic*, refers to the aorta, the main artery that a cardiologist would encounter in his/her work. As students spell each word, write it on the board. Ask them to cross-check their spelling with yours and correct any errors. Then use the list to brainstorm more words that share a spelling pattern, such as the following:

- *acrid*: slid, outdid, bid, Madrid, eyelid, rigid

- *tragic*: chronic, critic, epic, lyric, ethnic (*-ick* makes the same sound)

Day 4: Linkage

Tell students to see how many words they can find in the chain of letters on the Linkage Word Strips reproducible (page 127). The chain includes weekly words, as well as other words. See who can find the most words and discuss the words that students think are interesting. You might ask students to write on the board the most unusual word they found.

Day 5: Word Smart

Ask students to arrange the week's words across the top of their desks with plenty of workspace below. Have them respond to your questions by picking up the correct word card(s) and holding it so you can see the answer. If there are more than two correct answers, tell students to show only two—one in each hand. Ask: *Can you find . . .*

- a word that names an occupation?

- a word used in informal written or spoken language?

- a word hiding what a river does? (*flowers*)

- a word hiding a vehicle? (*cardiology*)

- a word that has a word part that means "human"?

- a word that contains an apostrophe?

- a word that has a word part that means "mind"?

- a word with a word part that means "the study of"?

- a word represented by a rose, daffodil, gladiola, or hydrangea?

- a word hiding a shooting star? (*meteorology*)

- a word hiding one out of a deck of 52? (*cardiologist*)

- a word with a word part that means "race"?

- a word with a word part that means "skin"?

- a word with a word part that means "heart"?

- a word that sounds similar to the word that refers to something you might do to a door?

- a word that is a contraction?

- a word hiding something you might have on your doorstep? (*dermatology*)

- a word that means "the study of the skin"?

- a word that is something that means "to stand for or act on behalf of something else"?

- a word that names a branch of anthropology?

- a word that names the study of the heart and its diseases?

- a word that names the study of humankind?

- a word that names the study of the mind and human behavior?

- a word that is the study of the atmosphere—weather and climate?

- a word hiding its opposite? (*couldn't*)

Ask students to arrange the *-ology* words from most important to least important to their lives and well being. Compare and discuss their arrangements.

Day 1: Meet the Words

This week's vocabulary is made up of 5 high-frequency words, 2 figures of speech, and 5 words that have the -cide suffix or cis base. Having a general knowledge of these words will be helpful. Begin by discussing the words and whether students have heard them before and in which context.

Have students pull apart the 12 word cards for this lesson and arrange them across the top of their desks. Then ask students to do the following:

- Hold up each card as you pronounce the word on it.
- Look at the word, read it aloud, and spell it with you.
- Return the word card to the top of their desk.

Provide a definition as necessary and share some of the word's features, as described below.

* **describe**: high-frequency word; verb usage; word part *scribe* means "to write or draw"; 2 syllables

* **although**: high-frequency word that is frequently misspelled; tricky spelling with one *l* (not two!) and *-ough* making a long-*o* sound; conjunction usage; 2 syllables

* **belief**: high-frequency word; tricky spelling with *i* before *e*, as in *believe*; noun usage; 2 syllables

* **another**: high-frequency word; adjective ("I want another biscuit.") and noun ("Children in a military family go to one school and then another.") usage; 3 syllables

* **beneath**: high-frequency word; adverb ("One bunk is above, and one is beneath.") and preposition ("The troll hid beneath the bridge.") usage; 2 syllables

* **onomatopoeia**: a figure of speech where the pronunciation of a word imitates its sound, as in *cuckoo*, *boom*, *zip*, and *pow*; 6 syllables

* **personification**: a figure of speech in which human characteristics (notice the word *person*) are given to an animal or a non-living object ("The night crept in slowly and pulled its dark cloak to cover the city."); 6 syllables

* **herbicide**: means "a substance used to kill plants, especially weeds"; *herb* means "plant," and *cide* is a word part that means "to kill"; 3 syllables

* **insecticide**: means "a substance used to kill insects"; 4 syllables

* **bactericide**: means "a substance used to kill bacteria"; 5 syllables

* **scissors**: means "an instrument with two blades used for cutting"; often misspelled; word part *cis* means "to cut"; 2 syllables

* **incision**: means "a cut or gash, often for surgical purposes"; 3 syllables

Day 2: Word Combo

Challenge students to complete each sentence with a word that is a combination of word parts from each of the words listed below it. Each word must contain the number of letters shown beside the sentence. Discuss the meanings of some of the common word parts that students combined to make the new words.

1. An _ _ _ _ _ _ _ _ is always a number. (8)
   potent/extended/permanent   (answer: *exponent*)

2. We made a huge _ _ _ _ _ _ _ _ _ . (9)
   beauty/disbelief/recovered   (answer: *discovery*)

3. The _ _ _ _ _ _ _ _ was ruthless. (8)
   potatoes/prediction/doctor   (answer: *dictator*)

4. The _ _ _ _ _ _ _ _ _ _ are right for rain. (10)
   indicate/auctions/conceited   (answer: *conditions*)

5. We will soon _ _ _ _ _ _ _ _ _ what to do. (9)
   illumine/counter/defraud   (answer: *determine*)

Day 3: Word Builder

Have students separate the letters at the bottom of this week's word template. Ask them to spell words as you call them out. Call out words in the order shown below. The final word should answer the following clue: The branches of the trees reached for the sky. (*personification*)

confine

conspire

inspire

inscription

infection

inspection

incision

snoop

notice

notion

option

point

friction

forensic

precision

proficient

poet

poetic

person

personification

Discuss any new words and their meanings. Point out the many -ion suffixes at the end the nouns. Note the *cis* in *precision*. Does that relate to the word part *cis* meaning "to cut"? Share that *script* in *inscription* means "written." Also, ask students how the word part *person* relates to *personification*. As students spell each word, write it on the board. Ask them to cross-check their spelling with yours and correct any errors.

Day 4: Linkage

Tell students to see how many words they can find in the chain of letters on the Linkage Word Strips reproducible (page 127). The chain includes weekly words, as well as other words. See who can find the most words and discuss the words that students think are interesting. You might ask students to write on the board the most unusual word they found.

Day 5: Word Smart

Ask students to arrange the week's words across the top of their desks with plenty of workspace below. Have them respond to your questions by picking up the correct word card(s) and holding it so you can see the answer. If there are more than two correct answers, tell students to show only two—one in each hand. Ask: *Can you find . . .*

- a word with a word part that means "to cut"?
- a word hiding a bug? (*insecticide*)
- a word that names something you shouldn't run with?
- a word that is a conjunction?
- a word represented by the purr of an engine, the panting of a locomotive, or the gentle touch of a branch?
- a word with a word part that means "to kill"?
- a word with a word part that means "written or drawn"?
- a word that is a preposition?
- a word part that means "germs"?
- a word that means "a substance used to kill bugs"?
- a word that means "a substance used to kill germs"?
- a word hiding something that movie stars do? (*bactericide*)
- a word with 3 consecutive letters we don't hear?
- a word that means "a substance used to kill plants or weeds"?
- a word that refers to something that someone thinks is true?
- a word that is a figure of speech?
- a word that is represented by *pow, bam, sizzle, purr, plop,* and *rattle*?
- a word with more than 3 syllables?
- a word that, if you changed the first letter to an *r*, would mean that you could relax?
- a word with a suffix that shows it is a noun?
- a words that ends in a vowel?
- a word with the greatest number of syllables?
- a word hiding a possessive pronoun? (*herbicide*)

Now ask students to return the words to the top of their desks. Their next challenge is to sort the words by a common characteristic. Then have partners share their work by asking each other, "What's my rule?" The guesses may include valid categories, but the correct answer is the partner's rule. Here are some sample categories for this week's words:

- *although, another, onomatopoeia, insecticide, incision* (words that begin with a vowel)
- *describe, although, belief, beneath, scissors* (words with 2 syllables)
- *herbicide, insecticide, bactericide* (words that rhyme)

Day 1: Meet the Words

This week's vocabulary is made up of high-frequency words and words that are derived from someone's name. Having a general knowledge of these words will be helpful. Begin by discussing the words and whether students have heard them before and in which context.

Have students pull apart the 12 word cards for this lesson and arrange them across the top of their desks. Then ask students to do the following:

*   Hold up each card as you pronounce the word on it.
*   Look at the word, read it aloud, and spell it with you.
*   Return the word card to the top of their desk.

Provide a definition as necessary and share some of the word's features, as described below.

*   ✳ **breathe**: high-frequency word; frequently misspelled because of tricky *ea* combination making a long-*e* sound, and also final silent *e*; verb often confused with its noun counterpart, *breath*; means "to take in air"

*   ✳ **committee**: high-frequency word; frequently misspelled–remember double consonants: 2 *m*'s, 2 *t*'s, and 2 *e*'s; 3 syllables

*   ✳ **desert**: high-frequency word; frequently confused with *dessert*–remember that *dessert* is sweet and needs 2 sugars; *desert* is a heteronym (pronounced differently according to meaning and origin): with first syllable stressed is a noun meaning "an arid region," and with second syllable stressed is a verb meaning "to leave an obligation abruptly"; 2 syllables

*   ✳ **discussed**: high-frequency word; past tense of *discuss*; 2 syllables

*   ✳ **either**: high-frequency word; frequently misspelled due to *ei* combination making a long-*e* sound; when used as a subject, takes a singular verb as in, "Either brand of bread is good."; 2 syllables

*   ✳ **mesmerize**: word that originated with Frederick Mesmer, an Austrian physician, who practiced hypnotism; currently a verb meaning "to spellbind or fascinate"; 3 syllables

*   ✳ **valentine**: word that originated with St. Valentine, a Christian martyr in the third century A.D., whose feast day is February 14 which, according to Roman tradition, is when birds pair off to nest; currently a noun that means "a message or gift given to a loved one on Valentine's Day"; 3 syllables

*   ✳ **shrapnel**: word that originated with Henry Shrapnel, an English army artillery officer who invented the hollow projectile that showers bullets and fragments; currently means "shell fragments from bullets"; 2 syllables

*   ✳ **vandal**: word originated from Vandals, a Germanic tribe that ravaged Rome and Spain in the fifth century A.D.; currently means "someone who maliciously damages or steals property"; 2 syllables

*   ✳ **diesel** : word originated from Rudolph Diesel (1858–1913), a German auto engineer; currently refers to a type of gasoline and engine; tricky spelling with *ie* combination that makes long-*e* sound–remember the word *die*, which is something you don't want your engine to do!; 2 syllables

*   ✳ **Braille**: word originated with Louis Braille (1809–52), a French teacher of the blind (also blind himself), who devised a system of reading by touching a combination of raised dots on paper; currently refers to this type of reading; sometimes capitalized

*   ✳ **maverick**: word originated with Samuel Maverick (1803–70), a Texas pioneer who refused to brand his calves; currently refers to someone who takes an independent stand; 3 syllables

Day 2: Word Combo

Challenge students to complete each sentence with a word that is a combination of word parts from each of the words listed below it. Each word must contain the number of letters shown beside the sentence. Discuss the meanings of some of the common word parts that students combined to make the new words.

1. The child's fever would _ _ _ _ _ _ _ _ flu. (8)
    in<u>ex</u>plicable/<u>dict</u>ator/compassion<u>ate</u>   (answer: *indicate*)

2. Stella's grades were _ _ _ _ _ _ _ _ _ . (9)
    <u>c</u>ellular/<u>ex</u>plicable/cli<u>ent</u>   (answer: *excellent*)

3. Fire _ _ _ _ _ _ _ _ _ _ is essential. (10)
    rein<u>vent</u>/<u>pre</u>arranged/abra<u>sion</u>   (answer: *prevention*)

4. We are part of the _ _ _ _ _ _ _ _ . (8)
    dra<u>ma</u>/simplic<u>ity</u>/mar<u>jor</u>am   (answer: *majority*)

5. The piece of pie was _ _ _ _ _ _ _ _ _! (9)
    <u>hum</u>anity/<u>ongo</u>ing/court<u>eous</u>   (answer: *humongous*)

Day 3: Word Builder

Have students separate the letters at the bottom of this week's word template. Ask them to spell words as you call them out. Call out words in the order shown below. The final word should answer the following clue: If you get too many, you may get into trouble! (*valentines*)

vent	aisle	alien
invent	isle	even
invents	sail	event
invest	sale	nestle
vines	nine	enliven
veins	tennis	snivel
vein	evil	valentines
vain	veil	

Discuss any new words and their meanings. As students spell each word, write it on the board. Ask them to cross-check their spelling with yours and correct any errors. Point out the sets of homophones–*vein/vain, aisle/isle, sail/sale*. Provide a context for each set. Use the word *nine* to find other words that can be spelled using the same pattern: *define, jawline, divine, guideline, feline*.

Day 4: Linkage

Tell students to see how many words they can find in the chain of letters on the Linkage Word Strips reproducible (page 127). The chain includes weekly words, as well as other words. See who can find the most words and discuss the words that students think are interesting. You might ask students to write on the board the most unusual word they found.

Day 5: Word Smart

Ask students to arrange the week's words across the top of their desks with plenty of workspace below. Have them respond to your questions by picking up the correct word card(s) and holding it so you can see the answer. If there are more than two correct answers, tell students to show only two–one in each hand. Ask: *Can you find . . .*

- a word with three pairs of double letters?
- a word pronounced two different ways?
- a word that originated with a doctor who hypnotized people?
- a word that names a way of reading through touch?
- a word related to a day when birds paired to nest?
- a word that might be used in a newspaper story about a wounded soldier?

- a word hiding something that a bride or groom agrees to do at their wedding? (*committee*)
- a word that describes something you might give or get on February 14?
- a word that was once the name of a Germanic tribe?
- a word hiding something most people love to do at a holiday feast? (*breathe*)
- a word that means "to abandon"?
- a word that means "someone who destroys something of value"?
- a word used to describe a person who stands alone and does his or her "own thing"?
- a word that means "a dry, arid area"?
- a word that is in the past tense?
- a word that means "to spellbind or fascinate"?
- a word that originated with a German automotive engineer?
- a word that, if used as a subject, takes a singular verb?
- a word that means "talked or debated"?
- a word that refers to a group of people organized to complete a task?
- a word that, if you changed the first letter, could be something you might see on the beach?
- a word hiding something we all eventually do? (*diesel*)
- a word hiding three pronouns? (*either: I, he, her*)
- a word with a prefix that means "with or together"?
- a word that originated with a saint?

Now ask students to return the word cards to the top of their desks. Their next challenge is to sort the words by a common characteristic. Then have partners share their work by asking each other, "What's my rule?" The guesses may include valid categories, but the correct answer is the partner's rule. Here are some sample categories for this week's words:

- *breathe, desert, discussed, mesmerize* (words that are verbs)
- *desert, discussed, diesel* (words that begin with a *d*)
- *valentine, shrapnel, vandal* (words that begin with one of the last 10 letters of the alphabet)

Day 1: Meet the Words

This week's vocabulary is made up of high-frequency words and words that come from Roman and Greek mythology. Having a general knowledge of these words will be helpful. Begin by discussing the words and whether students have heard them before and in which context.

Have students pull apart the 12 word cards for this lesson and arrange them across the top of their desks. Then ask students to do the following:

- Hold up each card as you pronounce the word on it.
- Look at the word, read it aloud, and spell it with you.
- Return the word card to the top of their desk.

Provide a definition as necessary and share some of the word's features, as described below.

✳ **embarrassed**: high-frequency word; frequently misspelled—remember 2 r's and 2 s's; 3 syllables

✳ **enough**: high-frequency word; usage as adverb, interjection, adjective, and pronoun (no need to confuse students about these as they are familiar with the word in spoken and written language); tricky spelling with -ough and /f/ sound; 2 syllables

✳ **especially**: high-frequency word; often misspelled and given a slurred pronunciation; -ly suffix signals adverb usage; 4 syllables

✳ **everywhere**: high-frequency word; compound; adverb meaning "in all places"; 3 syllables

✳ **excellent**: high-frequency word; adjective usage meaning "extraordinary or superior"; 3 syllables

✳ **atlas**: from Greek mythology, Atlas was a character who was forced by Zeus to hold the world on his shoulders as punishment for choosing a side in battle; current use means "a reference book of maps from around the world"; 2 syllables

✳ **cereal**: derived from Ceres, a Roman goddess of agriculture, and, hence, grain crops; currently means "a grain that is commonly eaten for breakfast"; 3 syllables

✳ **hygiene**: derived from Hygeia, the Greek goddess of cleanliness and good health; currently means "a practice that is conducive to good health"—brushing teeth, bathing, and so on; 2 syllables

✳ **mentor**: from Greek mythology, Mentor was both friend and advisor to Odysseus and teacher to his son; today used to mean "a wise counselor or teacher"; 2 syllables

✳ **panacea**: derived from Panacea, the Roman goddess of healing; today used to mean "something that solves all problems or cures all ills"; 4 syllables

✳ **volcano**: derived from Vulcan, the Roman god of fire; means "a natural feature formed when steam and lava erupt from a vent in the earth's crust"; 3 syllables

✳ **electricity**: derived from Electra, the daughter of Agamemnon in Greek mythology; today means "an electric charge or current"; 5 syllables

Day 2: Word Combo

Challenge students to complete each sentence with a word that is a combination of word parts from each of the words listed below it. Each word must contain the number of letters shown beside the sentence. Discuss the meanings of some of the common word parts that students combined to make the new words.

1. Haley didn't mind being a _ _ _ _ _ _ _ _. (8)
   vertical/match/candlestick　　　(answer: *maverick*)

2. Tom's _ _ _ _ _ _ _ _ will take him places. (9)
   respectful/inactive/foretell　　　(answer: *intellect*)

3. The general made a _ _ _ _ _ _ _ decision. (8)
   lateral/aerobic/tactless　　　(answer: *tactical*)

4. You can accomplish anything you _ _ _ _ _ _ _. (7)
   engine/imitate/average　　　(answer: *imagine*)

5. The event was a _ _ _ _ _ _ _ success! (8)
   losses/admiral/cooperate　　　(answer: *colossal*)

Day 3: Word Builder

Have students separate the letters at the bottom of this week's word template. Ask them to spell words as you call them out. Call out words in the order shown below. The final word should answer the following clue: This often causes a red face. (*embarrassment*)

meet

meat

names

term

team

renters

embers

amber

barren

banter

absent

barter

smart

stammer

steam

stream

smear

master

meant

meter

members

membrane

embarrass

embarrassment

Discuss any new words and their meanings. As students spell each word, write it on the board. Ask them to cross-check their spelling with yours and correct any errors. Then use the list to brainstorm more words that share a spelling pattern, such as the following:

- *steam*: stream, beam, gleam, team, dream (-*eme* makes the same sound)

- *smear*: hear, dear, fear, spear, headgear (-*eer* and -*ere* make the same sound)

Day 4: Stump the Class

Give pairs or small groups time to work together to find relationships between and among this week's words. Once they have found a category into which several of the words fit, they should write the words in the circle on the Word Clusters reproducible (see page 128) and the category underneath. Allow time for each pair or group to share one set of their words and ask the rest of the class to guess the category. Even though the other students may suggest a legitimate category, only the presenters' category is the correct answer. The goal is to stump the rest of the class with a unique category. (You might discover categories that you can add to the Day 5 Word Smart activity.)

Day 5: Word Smart

Ask students to arrange the week's words across the top of their desks with plenty of workspace below. Have them respond to your questions by picking up the correct word card(s) and holding

it so you can see the answer. If there are more than two correct answers, tell students to show only two—one in each hand. Ask: *Can you find . . .*

- a word that is in the past tense?

- a word that originated with a character from Greek mythology who carried the world on his shoulders?

- a word hiding a group of male human beings? (*mentor*)

- a word hiding something you might cook in? (*panacea*)

- a word that names something you might have for breakfast?

- a word that makes an /f/ sound but has no *f* in it?

- a word that is a compound?

- a word hiding a verb that means "to do very well"? (*excellent*)

- a word that originated with the Greek goddess of agriculture?

- a word that originated with the Greek goddess of cleanliness and good health?

- a word that originated with a mythological character who was a good friend and advisor to Odysseus?

- a word that originated with a Roman goddess who cured all ills?

- a word that originated with the Roman god of fire?

- a word that originated with the daughter of Agamemnon, a character in Greek mythology?

- a word with more than 3 syllables?

- a word with 2 syllables?

- a word that means "outstanding"?

- a word that means "good health habits"?

- a word that refers to a coach?

- a word that refers to something that solves all problems?

- a word hiding a place where prisoners are kept? (*excellent*)

- a word hiding the opposite of *imaginary*? (*cereal*)

- a word hiding a large community with its own government? (*electricity*)

- a word that names a collection of maps?

Now ask students to return the words to the top of their desks. Their next challenge is to sort the words by a common characteristic. Then have partners share their work by asking each other, "What's my rule?" The guesses may include valid categories, but the correct answer is the partner's rule. Here are some sample categories for this week's words:

- *embarrassed, enough, especially, everywhere, excellent, electricity* (word that begin with *e*)

- *atlas, volcano* (You use one word to find the other word.)

Day 1: Meet the Words

This week's vocabulary is made up of high-frequency words and words that are derived from the French language. See how many of these your students are already familiar with. Begin by discussing the words and whether students have heard them before and in which context.

Have students pull apart the 12 word cards for this lesson and arrange them across the top of their desks. Then ask students to do the following:

- Hold up each card as you pronounce the word on it.
- Look at the word, read it aloud, and spell it with you.
- Return the word card to the top of their desk.

Provide a definition as necessary and share some of the word's features, as described below.

* **foreign**: high-frequency word; adjective meaning "related to another country" or "strange and unfamiliar"; evolved from a word meaning "out of doors"; tricky spelling with *ei* combination and silent *g*; 2 syllables

* **frighten**: high-frequency word; commonly misspelled due to silent *gh*; related to *fright* and *frightened*; means "to scare or terrify"; 2 syllables

* **height**: high-frequency word; commonly misspelled with only 3 sounds and 6 letters; noun meaning "distance upward"

* **himself**: high frequency word; pronoun; caution students not to use "hisself," which is not a word; 2 syllables

* **humorous**: high-frequency word; adjective meaning "funny"; 3 syllables

* **cliché**: from the French language; means "a trite, overused expression" ("All good things must come to an end."); the final *e* is accented; 2 syllables

* **ambience**: from the French language; means "the mood or tone of the environment," as in "With new paint, the room has such a cozy ambience."; 3 syllables

* **bizarre**: from the French language; means "unusual in style, appearance or character"; 2 syllables

* **brochure**: from the French language; means "pamphlet"; 2 syllables

* **entourage**: from the French language; means "a group of attendants or associates;" comes from the word *entour*, which means "to surround," as in "The singer travels with an entourage."; 3 syllables

* **impromptu**: from the French language; commonly used as adjective meaning "done without preparation, hurriedly," as in, "Giving the impromptu introduction made me nervous."; translates as "in readiness"; synonym for *extemporaneous*; 3 syllables

* **debris**: from the French language; noun meaning "the remains of something broken apart," as in "The tornado roared through town and left debris littering the streets."; 2 syllables

Day 2: Picture That

Ask students to choose 6 of this week's words and arrange those word cards across the top of their desks. Next, have them fold a sheet of paper lengthwise (hot-dog style) and then fold it into thirds to create 6 equal boxes. As you review the definitions and discuss each of the words in this lesson, students write the words they selected in one of the boxes. After the discussion, tell them to sketch a picture that will help them remember the meaning of the words they chose.

Day 3: Word Builder

Have students separate the letters at the bottom of this week's word template. Ask them to spell words as you call them out. Call out words in the order shown below. The final word should answer the following clue: Another French word that might be handy—even if it's inappropriate! (*malapropos*)

lap

slap

also

lamp

romp

roam

plasma

alarm

rooms

prom

promo

solar

soap

soar

pool

spool

palm

polar

prop

moral

amoral

proposal

apropos *(from the French language: means "appropriate"; final s is silent)*

malapropos *(from the French language: means "inappropriate"; Note: final s is silent)*

Discuss any new words and their meanings, including the mystery word which is likely new to your students. As students spell each word, write it on the board. Ask them to cross-check their spelling with yours and correct any errors. Use *moral/amoral* and *apropos/malapropos* to teach the prefixes *a-* and *mal-*. In *amoral*, the prefix *a-* means "not," as in *atypical* (not typical) and *apathy* (no emotion). In *malapropos*, the prefix *mal-* means "bad," as in *malpractice* (bad practice, usually medical or legal) and *maladjusted* (badly adjusted).

Day 4: Linkage

Tell students to see how many words they can find in the chain of letters on the Linkage Word Strips reproducible (page 127). The chain includes weekly words, as well as other words. See who can find the most words and discuss the words that students think are interesting. You might ask students to write on the board the most unusual word they found.

Day 5: Word Smart

Ask students to arrange the week's words across the top of their desks with plenty of workspace below. Have them respond to your questions by picking up the correct word card(s) and holding it so you can see the answer. If there are more than two correct answers, tell students to show only two—one in each hand. Ask: *Can you find . . .*

- a word hiding a word that means "to rule"? (*foreign*)

- a word that means "something that has broken apart"?

- a word hiding a number? (*frighten, height*)

- a word that means "without preparation"?

- a word that is often what the doctor wants to know, besides your weight?

- a word that is a pronoun?

- a word that names an overused word or phrase?

- a word that means "a pamphlet"?

- a word hiding a sound you make with your mouth closed? (*humorous*)

- a word hiding a word that means "anger"? (*entourage*)

- a word that means "from another country"?

- a word hiding something I might give you to write about? (*impromptu*)

- a word hiding a pronoun other than *I*? (*height*)

- a word hiding a word that means "fear"? (*frighten*)

- a word that means "associates or attendants"?

- a word that means "unusual or unfamiliar"?

- a word that refers to an outlandish style or occurrence?

- a word that ends with a long-*a* sound but has no *a*?

- a word that ends with a long-*e* sound but has no *e*?

- a word that means "the mood or tone of an environment"?

- a word hiding 2 letters together that are used when texting the words *you are*? (*brochure*)

- a word that is an adjective that means "funny"?

- a word that means "to scare"?

- a word hiding an important school dance? (*impromptu*)

Now ask students to return the words to the top of their desks. Their next challenge is to sort the words by a common characteristic. Then have partners share their work by asking each other, "What's my rule?" The guesses may include valid categories, but the correct answer is the partner's rule. Here are some sample categories for this week's words:

- *foreign, frighten, height, cliché, bizarre, brochure, entourage, debris* (words with silent letters)

- *foreign, humorous, bizarre, impromptu* (adjectives)

- all 12 words (words that begin with one of the first 10 letters of the alphabet)

Day 1: Meet the Words

This week's vocabulary is made up of high-frequency words and words that are of Spanish origin. Begin by discussing the words and whether students have heard them before and in which context.

Have students pull apart the 12 word cards for this lesson and arrange them across the top of their desks. Then ask students to do the following:

- Hold up each card as you pronounce the word on it.
- Look at the word, read it aloud, and spell it with you.
- Return the word card to the top of their desk.

Provide a definition as necessary and share some of the word's features, as described below.

✳ **hungry**: high-frequency word; often misspelled by adding an *a*, which is the spelling for the country of Hungary; 2 syllables

✳ **immediately**: high-frequency word; suffix *-ly* signals adverb usage; 5 syllables

✳ **its**: high-frequency word; commonly confused with *it's*; *it's* is a contraction for *it is*, and *its* (without the apostrophe) is the possessive form of *it*

✳ **knowledge**: high-frequency word; usually used as a noun; tricky spelling with silent *k* and *d*; 2 syllables

✳ **square**: high-frequency word; multiple meanings as noun, verb, and adjective; *q* and *u* always appear together as partners

✳ **cafeteria**: borrowed from Spanish; often misspelled: remember *cafe* first with an *e*; in Spanish, *café* means "coffee" and *teria* means "a place where something is done"–usually a business and came to mean "help yourself"; 5 syllables

✳ **chocolate**: borrowed from Spanish; from the Nahuatl Indian word *xocolatl* (*xococ* means "bitter" and *atl* means "water"; remember the second *o* in spelling and pronunciation; 3 syllables

✳ **hurricane**: derived from the Spanish word *huracan*; means "a dangerous storm that brews in the Atlantic Ocean"; 3 syllables

✳ **tornado**: derived from the Spanish word *tronada* (thunderstorm); means "a violent whirlwind storm that brews over land"; 3 syllables

✳ **canyon**: derived from the Spanish word *cañon*; means "a deep valley with steep sides"; 2 syllables

✳ **canoe**: derived from the Spanish word *canoa*; commonly misspelled with tricky *-oe* ending; noun ("We will paddle the canoe down the river.") and verb ("We will canoe to the landing.") usage; 2 syllables

✳ **avocado**: derived from Spanish; names a fruit also called alligator pear by some; 4 syllables

Day 2: Word Combo

Challenge students to complete each sentence with a word that is a combination of word parts from each of the words listed below it. Each word must contain the number letters given in the sentence. Discuss the meanings of some of the common word parts that students combined to make the new words.

1. **Food was _ _ _ _ _ _ _ _ after the harvest. (9)**
   master<u>ful</u>/re<u>plen</u>ish/beau<u>tify</u>   (answer: *plentiful*)

2. **Michael knew the _ _ _ _ _ _ _ _ _ for breaking the rules. (10)**
   assign<u>ment</u>/<u>pun</u>ters/child<u>ishly</u>   (answer: *punishment*)

3. **The _ _ _ _ _ _ _ _ _ _ was a new addition to the community. (11)**
   <u>divi</u>ders/concu<u>ssion</u>/<u>sub</u>tracting   (answer: *subdivision*)

4. **The driver took the _ _ _ _ _ _ _ to make the trip faster. (8)**
   walk<u>way</u>/<u>mo</u>bilize/accelera<u>tor</u>   (answer: *motorway*)

5. **They are _ _ _ _ _ _ _ _ _ the play to make a decision. (9)**
   <u>re</u>action/inter<u>view</u>/alar<u>ming</u>   (answer: *reviewing*)

Day 3: Word Builder

Have students separate the letters at the bottom of this week's word template. Ask them to spell words as you call them out. Call out words in the order shown below. The final word should answer the following clue: These occur mostly in the summer. (*hurricanes*)

cashier

search

reach

chase

chaser

race

racer

ruins

nurse

cure

insure

incur

recur

share

shear

churn

siren

crier

cries

rush

crush

curse

rich

riches

richer

rerun

ranch

rancher

hurricanes

Discuss any new words and their meanings. As students spell each word, write it on the board. Ask them to cross-check their spelling with yours and correct any errors. Then use the list to brainstorm more words that share a spelling pattern, such as the following:

- *chase*: base, showcase, space, bookcase, case (-*ace* may also make this sound)

- *rush*: slush, hush, mush, blush, toothbrush, plush

Day 4: Stump the Class

Give pairs or small groups time to work together to find relationships between and among this week's words. Once they have found a category into which several of the words fit, they should write the words in the circle on the Word Clusters reproducible (see page 128) and the category underneath. Allow time for each pair or group to share one set of their words and ask the rest of the class to guess the category. Even though the other students may suggest a legitimate category, only the presenters' category is the correct answer. The goal is to stump the rest of the class with a unique category. (You might discover categories that you can add to the Day 5: Word Smart activity.)

Day 5: Word Smart

Ask students to arrange the week's words across the top of their

desks with plenty of workspace below. Have them respond to your questions by picking up the correct word card(s) and holding it so you can see the answer. If there are more than two correct answers, tell students to show only two—one in each hand. Ask: *Can you find . . .*

- a word that names a dangerous storm?

- a word hiding a word that means "to settle a dispute"? (*im<u>mediate</u>ly*)

- a word with a suffix that shows it is an adverb?

- a word hiding the opposite of *yes*? (*k<u>no</u>wledge*)

- a word hiding a pronoun other than *I*? (*im<u>me</u>diately*)

- a word that names something made with cacao beans?

- a word that is a pronoun?

- a word that names a shape that has four equal sides?

- a word that names a deep valley with steep sides?

- a word hiding a word that means "ripped"? (*<u>tor</u>nado*)

- a word hiding something that you might find on a kitchen shelf? (*<u>can</u>yon*)

- a word hiding the antonym for *early*? (*choco<u>late</u>*)

- a word hiding a small restaurant? (*<u>cafe</u>teria*)

- a word hiding the opposite of *later*? (*k<u>now</u>ledge*)

- a word with 5 syllables?

- a word that names a special style of boat?

- a word that ends in a vowel?

- a word that names a fruit?

- a word that refers to a vicious whirlwind?

- a word that names how we may feel just before lunch?

- a word that means "at once"?

Now ask students to return the words to the top of their desks. Their next challenge is to sort the words by a common characteristic. Then have partners share their work by asking each other, "What's my rule?" The guesses may include valid categories, but the correct answer is the partner's rule. Here are some sample categories for this week's words:

- *hurricane, tornado, canyon, avocado* (words that name something you might find in nature)

- *hungry/immediately, tornado/avocado* (word pairs that rhyme)

- *cafeteria, chocolate, canyon, canoe* (words that begin with a *c*)

Day 1: Meet the Words

This week's vocabulary is made up of high-frequency words and words that are of Arabic, Italian, or German in origin and are commonly used in the English language. Begin by discussing the words and whether students have heard them before and in which context.

Have students pull apart the 12 word cards for this lesson and arrange them across the top of their desks. Then ask students to do the following:

- Hold up each card as you pronounce the word on it.
- Look at the word, read it aloud, and spell it with you.
- Return the word card to the top of their desk.

Provide a definition as necessary and share some of the word's features, as described below.

* **necessary**: high-frequency word; adjective that means "essential"; tricky spelling: one *c* and two *s*'s; 4 syllables
* **neighbor**: high-frequency word; often misspelled because of *ei* combination and silent *gh*; Old English word part *neah*, which meant "near" and *gebur*, which meant "dwelling" ("A neighbor lives near our home."); 2 syllables
* **ourselves**: high-frequency word; plural pronoun; 2 syllables
* **once**: high-frequency word; often misspelled; usage as noun, adjective, adverb, and conjunction (There is no need to worry about the distinction as this is a common word.)
* **people**: high-frequency word; often misspelled with the *eo* making the long-*e* sound; 2 syllables
* **alcohol**: derived from the Arabic word *al-kuhul* (*al* means "the"); means "a solvent used in many products–lotions, beverages, colognes, and rubbing compounds"; 3 syllables
* **magazine**: derived from an Arabic word *makhazin*, which means "storehouse; originally meant "a warehouse for artillery" and then became "a warehouse of information (a published periodical)"; 3 syllables
* **colonel**: derived from an Italian word; often misspelled with -*olo* making an -*er* sound; means "the rank of an officer in the armed services"; also was a title of honor given to gentlemen in the South at one time; 2 syllables
* **incognito**: from the Italian word *incognito* meaning "unknown"; in current usage, means "having one's identity concealed"; adjective and adverb usage; 4 syllables
* **alfresco**: from the Italian language; translates as "in the coolness" but used to mean "outside in the fresh air"; used often in relation to dining at cafes and restaurants; adjective (alfresco café) and adverb (dining alfresco) usage; 3 syllables
* **hamburger**: derived from German; beef patty sandwich that may have originated in Hamburg, Germany; 3 syllables
* **schema**: derived from the German word; means "a plan or a conceptual understanding," as in "All of our reading has helped us build a schema for better understanding the Renaissance Period."; related to *scheme*; 2 syllables

Day 2: Word Combo

Challenge students to complete each sentence with a word that is a combination of word parts from each of the words listed below it. Each word must contain the number letters given in the sentence. Discuss the meanings of some of the common word parts that students combined to make the new words.

1. Look at the _ _ _ _ _ _ _ on this leaf. (7)
   tar**dy**/**la**bel/**bug**gy   (answer: *ladybug*)

2. The hungry dog was _ _ _ _ _ _ _ _ _ _. (10)
   ero**sive**/**ag**riculture/pro**gress**   (answer: *aggressive*)

3. In our word study, we talk about _ _ _ _ _ _ _ _. (8)
   acro**nyms**/**an**imated/**to**bacco   (answer: *antonyms*)

4. Everyone was _ _ _ _ _ _ _ _ after we won the championship. (8)
   bizarre/**ju**venile/gal**lant**   (answer: *jubilant*)

5. Mom will fix us a _ _ _ _ _ _ _ _ when we get home. (8)
   bevy/dam**age**/cov**er**   (answer: *beverage*)

Day 3: Word Builder

Have students separate the letters at the bottom of this week's word template. Ask them to spell words as you call them out. Call out words in the order shown below. The final word should answer the following clue: Another word derived from Arabic that sounds like it might hurt! (*artichokes*)

shortcake
hotcake
risk
racket
rocket
kites
sick
thick
thicker

actors

sheik

shriek

coast

ashore

score

hiker

earth

heart

heroic

ethics

shock

shocker

sticker

stroke

choke

artichokes

Discuss any new words and their meanings. Point out that an artichoke is a vegetable and is an Arabic word that has been adapted in the English language. *Sheik*, which refers to the patriarch of a family or tribe, is also an Arabic word. As students spell each word, write it on the board. Ask them to cross-check their spelling with yours and correct any errors. Then use the list to brainstorm more words that share a spelling pattern, such as the following:

- *ashore*: ignore, implore, sore, swore, more (-or makes the same sound)

- *choke*: poke, awoke, stroke, spoke, yoke, broke (-oak makes the same sound)

Day 4: Linkage

Tell students to see how many words they can find in the chain of letters on the Linkage Word Strips reproducible (page 127). The chain includes weekly words, as well as other words. See who can find the most words and discuss the words that students think are interesting. You might ask students to write on the board the most unusual word they found.

Day 5: Word Smart

Ask students to arrange the week's words across the top of their desks with plenty of workspace below. Have them respond to your questions by picking up the correct word card(s) and holding it so you can see the answer. If there are more than two

correct answers, tell students to show only two—one in each hand. Ask: *Can you find . . .*

- a word hiding a sound that a horse might make? (*neighbor*)

- a word that means "essential"?

- a word that is a plural pronoun?

- a word for something you might read?

- a word that means "outdoors"?

- a word hiding a possessive pronoun? (*ourselves*)

- two words: one is where you might eat and the other is what you might eat there?

- a word that refers to a solvent in many products?

- a word with the most syllables?

- a word that names a food with a word part that isn't an ingredient?

- a word that started as "near dwelling"?

- a word that is Arabic in origin?

- a word that is Italian in origin?

- a word that is German in origin?

- a word that means "hiding one's identity"?

- a word that has an /s/ sound?

- a word that goes before *twice*?

- a word with a silent *l*?

- a word with a silent *gh*?

- a word named after the town where it originated?

- a word that, if you're in witness protection, refers to how you might travel?

- a word that refers to someone you might salute?

- a word that refers to humans?

- a word that means "a plan or a collection of knowledge"?

- a word that can mean "a warehouse of weapons"?

- a word with 2 different letters making the same sound?

- a word with 1 syllable?

Now ask students to return the words to the top of their desks. Their next challenge is to sort the words by a common characteristic. Then have partners share their work by asking each other, "What's my rule?" The guesses may include valid categories, but the correct answer is the partner's rule. Here are some sample categories for this week's words:

- *neighbor, ourselves, alcohol, colonel, hamburger* (people and things you might see at a café)

- *once, incognito, alfresco* (words that begin and end with a vowel)

- *neighbor, ourselves, colonel* (words that are a subset of *people*)

Lesson 31

Day 1: Meet the Words

This week's vocabulary is made up of high-frequency words and words that are vivid adjectives describing appearances. These words may help students to write better descriptive pieces.

Have students pull apart the 12 word cards for this lesson and arrange them across the top of their desks. Then ask students to do the following:

- Hold up each card as you pronounce the word on it.
- Look at the word, read it aloud, and spell it with you.
- Return the word card to the top of their desk.

Provide a definition as necessary and share some of the word's features, as described below.

* **receive**: high-frequency word; often misspelled; *ei* combination—remember *i* before e except after *c*; verb usage; 2 syllables

* **recommend**: high-frequency word; tricky spelling, with one *c* and two *m*'s; verb meaning "to present as favorable"; 3 syllables

* **separate**: high-frequency word; tricky spelling—remember the two *a*'s are "separated" by an *r*; 3 syllables

* **themselves**: high-frequency word; plural pronoun; 2 syllables

* **usually**: high-frequency word; often misspelled—remember all 4 syllables when spelling to help include all vowels; adverb usage signaled by *-ly* ending

* **elegant**: strong adjective for describing appearance; means "refined and tasteful"; 3 syllables

* **distinct**: strong adjective for describing appearance; means "clearly different and separate" or "easy to hear, see, smell, or understand"; 2 syllables

* **rugged**: strong adjective for describing appearance; means "unpolished, unrefined, and rough"; 2 syllables

* **glamorous**: strong adjective for describing appearance; means "fascinating or beautiful in a showy way"; 3 syllables

* **grotesque**: strong adjective for describing appearance; means "fantastically ugly or bizarre"; ends with a /k/ sound; 2 syllables

* **unsightly**: strong adjective for describing appearance; means "distasteful or unpleasant to look at"; *-ly* suffix does not signal adverbial usage; 3 syllables

* **shadowy**: strong adjective for describing appearance; means "mysterious, enveloped in shadows"; 3 syllables

Day 2: Word Combo

Challenge students to complete each sentence with a word that is a combination of word parts from each of the words listed below it. Each word must contain the number letters given in the sentence. Discuss the meanings of some of the common word parts that students combined to make the new words.

1. What _ _ _ _ _ _ _ _ _ _ news! (10)
   studied/hazardous/pendulum   (answer: *stupendous*)

2. Coming in from the storm, the collie was _ _ _ _ _ _ _ _ _. (9)
   sightseers/unarguable/entirely   (answer: *unsightly*)

3. Abraham Lincoln's features were _ _ _ _ _ _ _ _ _ _ _. (11)
   extinction/disappointed/positive   (answer: *distinctive*)

4. Hannah remained _ _ _ _ _ _ _ _ _ _ as he walked toward her. (10)
   motorist/interaction/blameless   (answer: *motionless*)

5. The librarian had a _ _ _ _ _ _ _ _ _ manner. (9)
   generally/credential/confused   (answer: *congenial*)

Day 3: Word Builder

Have students separate the letters at the bottom of this week's word template. Ask them to spell words as you call them out. Call out words in the order shown below. The final word should answer the following clue: This is an adjective that describes a person who is thoughtful and sensitive to others' needs. (*considerate*)

increase

coarse

decorates

reacted

reactions

actions

retain

creation

canoe

canoeist

ocean

orient

dancer

senior

entries

certain

stained

saint

senator

steroid

secretion

enticed

consider

considerate

Discuss any new words and their meanings. As students spell each word, write it on the board. Ask them to cross-check their spelling with yours and correct any errors. Then use the list to brainstorm more words that share a spelling pattern, such as the following:

- *retain*: constrain, remain, pain, stain, grain, rain

- *saint*: acquaint, restraint, complaint, paint, faint

Day 4: Stump the Class

Give pairs or small groups time to work together to find relationships between and among this week's words. Once they have found a category into which several of the words fit, they should write the words in the circle on the Word Clusters reproducible (see page 128) and the category underneath. Allow time for each pair or group to share one set of their words and ask the rest of the class to guess the category. Even though the other students may suggest a legitimate category, only the presenters' category is the correct answer. The goal is to stump the rest of the class with a unique category. (You might discover categories that you can add to the Day 5: Word Smart activity.)

Note: For this week's words, you might want to give students more freedom to use other words besides the vocabulary lists to give clues about a character they feel fits one of the descriptive adjectives. They might give movie or book titles, dialogue, or other hints to help their classmates guess the character's name.

Day 5: Word Smart

Ask students to arrange the week's words across the top

of their desks with plenty of workspace below. Have them respond to your questions by picking up the correct word card(s) and holding it so you can see the answer. If there are more than two correct answers, tell students to show only two—one in each hand. Ask: *Can you find . . .*

- a word hiding something on the floor? (*rug*ged)

- a word hiding a group of males? (re*com*mend)

- a word hiding something at the bottom of a skirt or pants? (*them*selves)

- a word that means "clearly separate"?

- a word that means "unpleasant or unattractive"?

- a word with an ending that should make it an adverb—but doesn't?

- a word that is a plural pronoun?

- a word hiding a slang word for *showy*? (*glam*orous)

- a word that is a pronoun or is hiding a pronoun other than *I*?

- a word that ends with a /k/ but has no *k*?

- a word hiding something that follows you closely? (*shadow*y)

- a word that refers to something you might have to do to children who are fighting?

- a word that, if you changed the prefix, would mean "gone forever"?

- a word that means "to get"?

- a word hiding a synonym for *vision*? (un*sight*ly)

- a word hiding something you do when you're tired and you exhale? (un*sigh*tly)

- a word that is an antonym for *refined*?

- a word that means "beautiful or showy"?

- a word that means "refined"?

- a word that is a synonym for *hideous*?

- a word that refers to something you want people to do for you when you look for a job?

- a word with a prefix that means "not"?

- a word hiding a word that means "to praise"? (re*commend*)

Ask students to take their descriptive words and arrange them from most to least desirable characteristics. Compare their opinions and discuss as time allows.

Day 1: Meet the Words

This week's vocabulary is made up of high-frequency words and words that are adjectives describing sizes. These words may help students to write better descriptive pieces.

Have students pull apart the 12 word cards for this lesson and arrange them across the top of their desks. Then ask students to do the following:

• Hold up each card as you pronounce the word on it.

• Look at the word, read it aloud, and spell it with you.

• Return the word card to the top of their desk.

Provide a definition as necessary and share some of the word's features, as described below.

✳ **though**: high-frequency word; often misspelled because -ough makes a long-o sound; often confused with thought and through; usually used as a conjunction to mean "although," but can be used as adverb meaning "however"

✳ **thought**: high-frequency word; often misspelled and confused with though, and through; usage as noun meaning "mental activity" and as a verb (past tense of think); -ought spelling pattern used for words like sought, fought, bought

✳ **through**: high-frequency word; often misspelled and confused with though, and thought; pay careful attention to the thr- blend at the beginning; homophone for threw; usage as preposition ("through the passage"), adjective ("She's through with his selfish ways.") and adverb ("I'm just passing through.")

✳ **throughout**: high-frequency word; often misspelled because of -ough combination; usage as preposition and adverb; 2 syllables

✳ **you're**: high-frequency word; often confused with your although the pronunciation is slightly different (enunciate the difference for students); contraction for you are

✳ **your**: high-frequency word; often confused with you're although the pronunciation is slightly different; possessive pronoun

✳ **diminutive**: adjective that describes size; means "tiny," as in "The singer was diminutive but had a mighty voice."; related to diminish; 4 syllables

✳ **colossal**: adjective that describes size; means "gigantic," as in, "The officer's colossal presence made everyone fearful."; 3 syllables

✳ **enormous**: adjective that describes size; means "huge"; 3 syllables

✳ **microscopic**: adjective that describes size; means "very tiny so as to be almost invisible"; word part micro means "small," and scopic means "to look"; related to microscope, which allows one to see extraordinarily small objects; 4 syllables

✳ **voluminous**: adjective that describes size; means "of great size or fullness"; related to volume; 4 syllables

✳ **immense**: adjective that describes size; means "vast and immeasurable"; word part mense means "to measure" and prefix im- means "not" = "not to be measured"; 2 syllables

Day 2: Word Combo

Challenge students to complete each sentence with a word that is a combination of word parts from each of the words listed below it. Each word must contain the number letters given in the sentence. Discuss the meanings of some of the common word parts that students combined to make the new words.

1. I _ _ _ _ _ _ _ _ _ between happiness and sadness when I watch this movie. (9)
   or<u>nate</u>/<u>al</u>ready/chat<u>ter</u>   (answer: alternate)

2. The noise didn't _ _ _ _ _ _ _ _ after the teacher came in the room. (8)
   <u>e</u>stablish/legis<u>late</u>/<u>ca</u>dets   (answer: escalate)

3. The people are threatening to _ _ _ _ _ _ _ _ their ruler. (9)
   <u>o</u>mit/fe<u>ver</u>/<u>throw</u>away   (answer: overthrow)

4. The tree's shadow was _ _ _ _ _ _ _ as the sun set. (8)
   <u>g</u>ander/<u>gi</u>ants/acroba<u>tic</u>   (answer: gigantic)

5. That actress has a _ _ _ _ _ _ _ personality. (8)
   ethi<u>c</u>/<u>mag</u>azine/<u>net</u>working   (answer: magnetic)

Day 3: Word Builder

Have students separate the letters at the bottom of this week's word template. Ask them to spell words as you call them out. Call out words in the order shown below. The final word should answer the following clue: This is another little adjective! (miniature)

aim

name

mute

aunt

auntie

earn

airtime

minute

minuet

tinier

ruin

item

emit

untie

unit

unite

remit

tear

tier

irate

inertia

miniature

Discuss any new words and their meanings. Point out that *minute* (a heteronym with stress on the second syllable that means "tiny"), *tiny/tinier*, and *irate* might also be used to describe someone or something. As students spell each word, write it on the board. Ask them to cross-check their spelling with yours and correct any errors. Then use the list to brainstorm more words that share a spelling pattern, such as the following:

- *name*: shame, blame, frame, inflame, fame (*-aim* makes the same sound)

- *irate*: collate, mate, gate, fixate, infiltrate, state

Day 4: Linkage

Tell students to see how many words they can find in the chain of letters on the Linkage Word Strips reproducible (page 127). The chain includes weekly words, as well as other words. See who can find the most words and discuss the words that students think are interesting. You might ask students to write on the board the most unusual word they found.

Day 5: Word Smart

Ask students to arrange the week's words across the top of their desks with plenty of workspace below. Have them respond to your questions by picking up the correct word card(s) and holding it so you can see the answer. If there are more than two correct

answers, tell students to show only two—one in each hand. Ask: *Can you find . . .*

- a word that means "huge"?

- a word that means "tiny"?

- a word that means "almost invisible"?

- a word with a word part that means "to measure"?

- a word that is a contraction?

- a word hiding the opposite of *gain*? (*colossal*)

- a word hiding this missing word: *either-or* and *neither-___?* (*enormous*)

- a word that is a possessive pronoun?

- a word hiding the word that means "should"? (*thought*)

- a word hiding the abbreviation for *minute*? (*diminutive*)

- a word that relates to volume?

- a word that translates to mean "not to be measured or immeasurable"?

- a word that can be used as a preposition?

- a word that can used as an adverb or a conjunction?

Have students put the word cards for *though, thought, through,* and *throughout* in their workspace. Ask them to pick up the word you call out as quickly as possible and hold it up for you to see. Then call out these words at random so that students will notice the slight differences among them. Have students put those word cards aside.

Ask them to place the word cards for *you're* and *your* in their workspace. Have them hold up the card for each word as you say it. Be careful to enunciate the words clearly. Do this rapidly a few times. Then, use each word in a sentence and have students hold up the word card that completes it.

- Please bring __ dog over to play with mine.

- ___ the best friend anyone could have!

- I hope ___ chosen to be our class president.

- Is that __ book on the floor?

Now ask students to put aside those word cards and put all the descriptive words in their workspace. Let them work with a partner to decide on someone or something from a comic strip or a TV show that they could use these words to describe. You may want to caution them not to use them as personal references for anyone in the school.

Day 1: Meet the Words

This week's vocabulary is made up of high-frequency words, a figure of speech, and words that are commonly used on employment applications.

Have students pull apart the 12 word cards for this lesson and arrange them across the top of their desks. Then ask students to do the following:

- Hold up each card as you pronounce the word on it.
- Look at the word, read it aloud, and spell it with you.
- Return the word card to the top of their desk.

Provide a definition as necessary and share some of the word's features, as described below.

* **weight**: high-frequency word; often misspelled due to the *ei* combination, which makes a long-*a* sound and the silent *gh*; homophone for *wait*

* **where**: high-frequency word; often confused with *were*, although *where* has a distinct /hw/ sound.

* **seriously**: high-frequency word; adverb meaning "gravely," as in "Shep was seriously injured in the accident." or "earnestly," as in "I am seriously considering my future career options."; 4 syllables

* **quiet**: high-frequency word; often confused with *quite* and *quit*, even though all sounds in *quiet* are expressed; adjective usage; 2 syllables

* **oxymoron**: used often in language arts as a figure of speech; *oxy* means "sharp," and *moron* means "dull"; an oxymoron means "the combination of two words with opposite meanings," such as *bittersweet, deafening silence, new routine, fresh frozen, awfully good*; 4 syllables

* **applicant**: a common employment application word; means "the person who is applying for a job"; suffix -*ant* is usually added to verbs to make nouns and adjectives, as in *serve/ servant, please/pleasant, defend/defendant*; 3 syllables

* **employer**: a common employment application word; means "the person or business that someone works for"; suffix -*er* means "one who" [employs]; 3 syllables

* **permanent**: a common employment application word; means "existing for a long or indefinite period," as in "Are you looking for a permanent position with our company?"; 3 syllables

* **temporary**: a common employment application word; means "lasting only a limited time"; antonym for *permanent*; a temporary position with a company might be one filled during heavy periods of business, such as a tax business that has great volume in the late winter and early spring (through April 15); 4 syllables

* **chronological**: a common employment application word; means "arranged in order of time," as in "List your previous jobs in chronological order from first to present."; 5 syllables

* **dependents**: a common employment application word; usually used for tax purposes; means "The number of people who are dependent upon the applicant for a major portion of their financial support."; may include a spouse, children, parents, or other relatives; plural; 3 syllables

* **references**: a common employment application word; means "the people the applicant lists who would be willing to write to or speak with the employer to testify to the applicant's work habits and character"; references may be former or present employers, teachers, or anyone who has knowledge of the applicant's habits and character; usually relatives are not included as references, since they may be biased; 4 syllables

Day 2: Word Combo

Challenge students to complete each sentence with a word that is a combination of word parts from each of the words listed below it. Each word must contain the number letters given in the sentence. Discuss the meanings of some of the common word parts that students combined to make the new words.

1. Taking out the trash is a _ _ _ _ _ _ _ _ _ job. (9)
   unlikely/volumize/military   (answer: *voluntary*)

2. The school is _ _ _ _ _ _ _ _ _ _ _ my fees. (11)
   upgrading/threshold/withdrawal   (answer: *withholding*)

3. The high salary is a great _ _ _ _ _ _ _ _ . (9)
   combative/censorship/inappropriate   (answer: *incentive*)

4. Tamara is eager to do an _ _ _ _ _ _ _ _ _ _ at the retail store. (10)
   inactive/guardianship/midwestern   (answer: *internship*)

5. The _ _ _ _ _ _ _ _ _ are happy with their benefits. (9)
   seasonal/percussion/channel   (answer: *personnel*)

Day 3: Word Builder

Have students separate the letters at the bottom of this week's word template. Ask them to spell words as you call them out. Call out words in the order shown below. The final word should answer the following clue: These two words make a job even better! (*fringe benefits*)

infest

infesting

resting

refining

sniffing

sneering

festering

integer

resent

fifteen

tense

string

brief

infringe

intern

beginner

resign

benefits

fringe benefits

Discuss any new words and their meanings. As students spell each word, write it on the board. Ask them to cross-check their spelling with yours and correct any errors. Then use the list to brainstorm more words that share a spelling pattern, such as the following:

- *resent*: spent, accent, comment, present, fragment

- *resign*: sign, design, align, assign (*-ine* may also make this sound)

Day 4: Stump the Class

Give pairs or small groups time to work together to find relationships between and among this week's words. Once they have found a category into which several of the words fit, they should write the words in the circle on the Word Clusters reproducible (see page 128) and the category underneath. Allow time for each pair or group to share one set of their words and ask the rest of the class to guess the category. Even though the other students may suggest a legitimate category, only the presenters' category is the correct answer. The goal is to stump the rest of the class with a unique category. (You might discover categories that you can add to the Day 5: Word Smart activity.)

Day 5: Word Smart

Ask students to arrange the week's words across the top of their desks with plenty of workspace below. Have them respond to your questions by picking up the correct word card(s) and holding it so you can see the answer. If there are more than two correct answers, tell students to show only two—one in each hand. Ask: *Can you find . . .*

- words that are the opposite of each other?

- a word for a person who applies for a job?

- a word hiding something a mountain house might be made of? (*chrono<u>log</u>ical*)

- a word hiding a male? (*per<u>man</u>ent*)

- a word with a long-*a* sound but it has no *a*?

- a word that means "people who rely on a person for their financial support"?

- a word for the person or business that gives you a job?

- a word for people you depend on to speak well of you to a potential employer?

- a word that starts with a /hw/ sound?

- a word for "long lasting or indefinite"?

- a word for "limited time"?

- a word that you might see posted in a hospital or library?

- a word that means "in order of time"?

- a word that describes these phrases: "freezer burn" and "jumbo shrimp"?

- a word that fits in this sentence: "Playing too many video games __ affected his work."?

- a word that, without its suffix, would be a verb?

- a word with a word part that means "dull"?

- a word hiding a pronoun other than *I*? (*w<u>e</u>ight*)

- a word that is usually found on job applications?

If possible, you might have a job application ready for your students to fill out that would give them some idea of the vocabulary necessary to complete it. You can enter "job application" in your search engine and find many to choose from.

Day 1: Meet the Words

This week's vocabulary is made up of high-frequency words and words that are time related. These words may help students to write better descriptive pieces.

Have students pull apart the 12 word cards for this lesson and arrange them across the top of their desks. Then ask students to do the following:

- Hold up each card as you pronounce the word on it.
- Look at the word, read it aloud, and spell it with you.
- Return the word card to the top of their desk.

Provide a definition as necessary and share some of the word's features, as described below.

* **familiar**: high-frequency word; often misspelled—pay attention to each syllable; means "commonly known"; related to *family*; 4 syllables

* **favorite**: high-frequency word; don't forget silent *e* at end; 3 syllables

* **experience**: high-frequency word; commonly misspelled; noun ("Camping was a great experience!") and verb ("We will experience the impact of the hurricane soon.") usage; sometimes asked for on job applications and included on resumes to mean "jobs or encounters one has had that relate to the job"; 4 syllables

* **tendency**: high-frequency word; means "inclination toward something," as in "I have a tendency to overeat at Thanksgiving."; 3 syllables

* **ancient**: a time-related word; means "from a time long past, very old," as in "The ancient ruins of the arena were preserved for tourists to see."; 2 syllables

* **continual**: a time-related word; means "repeated, very frequent," as in "The continual rain left us unable to enjoy our vacation."; related to continue; 4 syllables

* **decade**: a time-related word; means "ten years, "as in, "Dad's clothes are from two decades ago!"; word part *dec* means "ten," as in a decagon, which has 10 angles and 10 sides; word part *deci* means "tenth," as in a decimal showing tenths; 2 syllables

* **intermittent**: a time-related word; means "stopping and starting at intervals," as in "The pain was intermittent, so Vincent was able to get some rest."; prefix *inter-* means "between"; related to *intermission*; 4 syllables

* **annual**: a time-related word; means "once a year"; Latin word *annus* means "year," related to *anniversary*; 3 syllables

* **periodic**: a time-related word; means "recurring at intervals," as in "periodic visits from my friend"; related to *period* and *periodically*; 4 syllables

* **sporadic**: a time-related word; means "random, scattered occurrences," as in sporadic outbreaks of flu; 3 syllables

* **lengthy**: a time-related word; means "of great length," as in a lengthy journey; 2 syllables

Day 2: Word Combo

Challenge students to complete each sentence with a word that is a combination of word parts from each of the words listed below it. Each word must contain the number letters given in the sentence. Discuss the meanings of some of the common word parts that students combined to make the new words.

1. The two signatures looked _ _ _ _ _ _ _ _ _. (9)
   beautiful/surgical/ideally/dental   (answer: *identical*)

2. I'm the _ _ _ _ _ _ _ _ of the play. (8)
   narrow/prosecutor/rabies   (answer: *narrator*)

3. Can you _ _ _ _ _ _ _ _ my parking sticker? (8)
   update/valuable/radical   (answer: *validate*)

4. I missed that problem because I _ _ _ _ _ _ _ _ two numbers. (8)
   berated/indirect/convertible   (answer: *inverted*)

5. Lou was _ _ _ _ _ _ _ _ _ _ _ of the extremely generous offer. (11)
   faithful/misbehave/trustworthy   (answer: *mistrustful*)

Day 3: Word Builder

Have students separate the letters at the bottom of this week's word template. Ask them to spell words as you call them out. Call out words in the order shown below. The final word should answer the following clue: This is a time-related word that describes part of a day. (*afternoons*)

reason

nonfat

often

soften

sonnet

front

fasten

fare

fears

safer

faster

snare

roost

roast

tones

sofa

nose

neon

stone

snore

foster

forest

frost

raft

afternoons

Discuss any new words and their meanings. As students spell each word, write it on the board. Ask them to cross-check their spelling with yours and correct any errors. Then use the list to brainstorm more words that share a spelling pattern, such as the following:

- *nonfat*: brat, cat, doormat, chitchat, that, format, cravat
- *stone*: throne, bone, tone, alone, birthstone, cyclone, phone

Day 4: Linkage

Tell students to see how many words they can find in the chain of letters on the Linkage Word Strips reproducible (page 127). The chain includes weekly words, as well as other words. See who can

find the most words and discuss the words that students think are interesting. You might ask students to write on the board the most unusual word they found.

Day 5: Word Smart

Ask students to arrange the week's words across the top of their desks with plenty of workspace below. Have them respond to your questions by picking up the correct word card(s) and holding it so you can see the answer. If there are more than two correct answers, tell students to show only two—one in each hand. Ask: *Can you find . . .*

- a word that relates to time?
- a word hiding a number? (*ten*dency)
- a word hiding someone who tells untruths? (fami*liar*)
- a word with a word part that means "ten"?
- a word that relates to unpredictable time?
- a word that means "ten years"?
- a word hiding something you find at the end of a sentence? (*period*ic)
- a word that means "an inclination toward something"?
- a word that means "very old"?
- a word hiding something you might get at a party? (*favor*ite)
- a word you might see on a job application?
- a word hiding something a baseball catcher needs? (inter*mitt*ent)
- a word that means "occurring regularly"?
- a word that means "known"?
- a word that means "yearly"?
- a word that, if you had a choice, would tell how often you want to get a cold?
- a word that begins with a vowel?
- a word that ends with a vowel?
- a word with 4 syllables?

Now, have students place all of the time-related word cards in their workspaces. Ask them to arrange the words from the one that occurs most frequently to the one that occurs least frequently. Discuss their choices.

Day 1: Meet the Words

This week's vocabulary is made up of high-frequency words and interesting adverbs that can make our writing livelier.

Have students pull apart the 12 word cards for this lesson and arrange them across the top of their desks. Then ask students to do the following:

- Hold up each card as you pronounce the word on it.
- Look at the word, read it aloud, and spell it with you.
- Return the word card to the top of their desk.

Provide a definition as necessary and share some of the word's features, as described below.

* **because**: high-frequency word; conjunction that signals a cause/effect relationship; 2 syllables

* **divergent**: high-frequency word; adjective that means "differing," as in "divergent ways of solving a problem"; the prefix di- generally means "two" (*discuss how that relates to divergent*); 3 syllables

* **Europe**: high-frequency word; one of the seven continents; includes the countries of France, Spain, and Italy; derived from a mythological character, Europa; capitalized; 2 syllables

* **ocean**: high-frequency word; frequently misspelled; remember the *ea* in the synonym *sea*; 2 syllables

* **adamantly**: adverb; -ly suffix signals adverb usage; means "unyieldingly," as in "adamantly opposed to wearing a uniform in school"; 4 syllables

* **anxiously**: adverb; -ly suffix signals adverb usage; means "eagerly," as in "anxiously awaiting my turn"; 3 syllables

Note: Except for the adjective *cowardly*, the suffix -ly in the following words signals adverb usage:

* **brazenly**: adverb; means "boldly," as in "The thief brazenly walked onstage before the crowd."; 3 syllables

* **casually**: adverb; means "unexpectedly, unintentionally or informally," as in "Selma casually walked past the boss without noticing him."; 4 syllables

* **cautiously**: adverb; means "with caution, care, and deliberation," as in "The detective cautiously entered the dark room."; 3 syllables

* **cowardly**: adjective; means "lacking courage," as in "the cowardly way Jason ran away from telling the truth"; 3 syllables

* **cynically**: adverb; means "distrusting the motives of others"; 4 syllables

* **eerily**: adverb; means "uncanny and weird," as in "The wolf's howls echoed eerily through the night"; 3 syllables

Day 2: Word Combo

Challenge students to complete each sentence with a word that is a combination of word parts from each of the words listed below it. Each word must contain the number letters given in the sentence. Discuss the meanings of some of the common word parts that students combined to make the new words.

1. There was a _ _ _ _ _ _ _ _ blast of noise from the ballgame. (9)
   unusual/bulletin/concisely   (answer: *continual*)
2. Ben has a job as _ _ _ _ _ _ _ _ _. (10)
   searching/reaction/accuser   (answer: *researcher*)
3. The countryside was marked with _ _ _ _ _ _ _ _ roads. (9)
   vertical/gentleman/dilute   (answer: *divergent*)
4. We will not _ _ _ _ _ _ _ tardiness. (8)
   capitol/berate/blazer   (answer: *tolerate*)
5. The letter of _ _ _ _ _ _ _ _ made Lucy more determined. (9)
   subject/receptor/sensation   (answer: *rejection*)

Day 3: Word Builder

Have students separate the letters at the bottom of this week's word template. Ask them to spell words as you call them out. Call out words in the order shown below. The final word should answer the following clue: This adverb describes doing things in a persistent and demanding way. (*insistently*)

list

listen

tiny

test

enlist

silent

style

stylist

stilts

testy

tinsel

inlet

sly

slyest

stint

nine

ninety

intently

insist

insistently

Discuss any new words and their meanings. As students spell each word, write it on the board. Ask them to cross-check their spelling with yours and correct any errors. Then use the list to brainstorm more words that share a spelling pattern, such as the following:

- *test*: best, nest, contest, west

- *stint*: print, flint, mint, sprint, tint, imprint, hint

Day 4: Stump the Class

Give pairs or small groups time to work together to find relationships between and among this week's words. Once they have found a category into which several of the words fit, they should write the words in the circle on the Word Clusters reproducible (see page 128) and the category underneath. Allow time for each pair or group to share one set of their words and ask the rest of the class to guess the category. Even though the other students may suggest a legitimate category, only the presenters' category is the correct answer. The goal is to stump the rest of the class with a unique category. (You might discover categories that you can add to the Day 5: Word Smart activity.)

Day 5: Word Smart

Ask students to arrange the week's words across the top of their desks with plenty of workspace below. Have them respond to your questions by picking up the correct word card(s) and holding it so you can see the answer. If there are more than two correct answers, tell students to show only two—one in each hand. Ask: *Can you find . . .*

- a word hiding something you do at the pool? (*divergent*)

- a word that means "weirdly"?

- a word that means "boldly"?

- a word hiding a farm animal? (*cowardly*)

- a word hiding something a beaver might build? (*adamantly*)

- a word hiding a word that means "everything"? (*casually*, *cynically*)

- a word that names a continent?

- a word that signals a relationship between events?

- a word that means "eagerly or nervously"?

- a word that means "informally or unintentionally?

- a word that means "carefully or suspiciously"?

- a word that means "distrustfully"?

- words that show the different sounds that *c* makes?

- a word with a prefix that means "two"?

- a word that is always capitalized?

- a word hiding something you might use for climbing? (*Europe*)

- a word that means "differing," as in opposite approaches to doing something?

- a word that describes what the lion was like before meeting the wizard?

- a word that means "unyieldingly"?

Have students arrange the adverbs in order from the most desirable characteristic to the least desirable characteristic. Discuss their choices. Remind them that these are good words to consider in their writing.

it's	index
questions	reference
problem	citation
complete	bibliography
caption	book

a e e n p p r s s w

Systematic Word Study for Grades 4–6 © 2011 by Cheryl M. Sigmon • Scholastic Teaching Resources • Lesson 1

since	accuracy
piece	acute
usually	computation
friends	obtuse
heard	quiz

a c i m n o o p s t t u

become	camouflage
across	carnivore
however	herbivore
happened	omnivore
adaptation	enemy

a a b e h i l o r v

Systematic Word Study for Grades 4–6 © 2011 by Cheryl M. Sigmon • Scholastic Teaching Resources • Lesson 3

whole	amendment
remember	document
early	constitution
reached	preamble
listen	jury

a e e e e i n p r r s t t v

cover	fable
several	genre
himself	metaphor
morning	simile
vowel	mystery

a c e e g i o r s t

Systematic Word Study for Grades 4–6 © 2011 by Cheryl M. Sigmon • Scholastic Teaching Resources • Lesson 5

true	composite
hundred	diameter
against	probability
pattern	quadrant
numeral	radius

a e e i l l n o s s t t

slowly	biome
voice	biosphere
cried	ecosystem
notice	ecology
south	muscle

a e e i l m n n n o r t v

Systematic Word Study for Grades 4–6 © 2011 by Cheryl M. Sigmon • Scholastic Teaching Resources • Lesson 7

ground	conjunction
I'll	judicial
figure	legislative
certain	executive
travel	phony

a c e g i l n n o o r s s

English	proofread
finally	quotations
wait	analogy
correct	alliteration
interjection	nightmare

a a e i i l l n o r t t

 Systematic Word Study for Grades 4–6 © 2011 by Cheryl M. Sigmon • Scholastic Teaching Resources • Lesson 9

quickly	convex
shown	exponent
verb	parallelogram
inches	vertex
street	nickname

a a a e g l l l m o p r r

decided	kinetic
course	chemical
surface	thermal
produce	mechanical
potential	crazy

e e e h m m o r r s t t

Systematic Word Study for Grades 4–6 © 2011 by Cheryl M. Sigmon • Scholastic Teaching Resources • Lesson 11

yet	revenue
government	annex
object	boycott
among	immigrant
cannot	paragraph

a g i i i i m m n o r t

machine	hyperbole
plane	idiom
system	superlative
brought	clause
understand	quarantine

a e e i l p r s s t u v

Systematic Word Study for Grades 4–6 © 2011 by Cheryl M. Sigmon • Scholastic Teaching Resources • Lesson 13

explain	inequality
though	ratio
language	volume
thousands	equilateral
equation	digits

a a e e i l l q r t u

carefully	eclipse
scientists	cholesterol
known	carcinogen
island	translucent
constellation	husband

a a a c c d i l o r r s u v

Systematic Word Study for Grades 4–6 © 2011 by Cheryl M. Sigmon • Scholastic Teaching Resources • Lesson 15

hostile	obnoxious
aggravated	resentful
belligerent	insensitive
arrogant	spiteful
callous	vindictive

a a b d e e e g i l r s

worthless	dejected
forlorn	depressed
lonesome	estranged
ostracized	humiliated
alienated	obsolete

d e e i n o p r s s

Systematic Word Study for Grades 4–6 © 2011 by Cheryl M. Sigmon • Scholastic Teaching Resources • Lesson 17

suddenly	amiable
direction	altruistic
anything	charitable
divided	empathetic
general	humane

a a b c e h i l r t

energy	ecstatic
subject	enthusiastic
region	elated
believe	gratified
exercise	vivacious

a   c   e   h   i   i   n   s   s   t   t   u

Systematic Word Study for Grades 4–6 © 2011 by Cheryl M. Sigmon • Scholastic Teaching Resources • Lesson 19

developed	monarchy
difference	anarchy
probably	aristocracy
written	autocracy
length	democracy
dictatorship	theocracy

a c d h i i o p r s t t

reason	cautioned
present	bellowed
beautiful	interrupted
edge	responded
sign	taunted
asserted	demanded

a   c   d   e   i   l   m   n   o   p

Systematic Word Study for Grades 4–6 © 2011 by Cheryl M. Sigmon • Scholastic Teaching Resources • Lesson 21

finished	imperialism
discovered	fascism
beside	communism
million	patriotism
lie	capitalism
perhaps	socialism

a   i   i   m   o   p   r   s   t   t

weather	aquaphobia
instruments	hemophobia
third	claustrophobia
include	astraphobia
built	optophobia
glossary	amaxophobia

a a a b c h h i n o o p r

Systematic Word Study for Grades 4–6 © 2011 by Cheryl M. Sigmon • Scholastic Teaching Resources • Lesson 23

represent	anthropology
whether	cardiology
clothes	ethnology
flowers	dermatology
teacher	meteorology
couldn't	psychology

a c d g i i l o o r s t

describe	personification
although	herbicide
belief	insecticide
another	bactericide
beneath	scissors
onomatopoeia	incision

a c e f i i i i n n o o p r s t

Systematic Word Study for Grades 4–6 © 2011 by Cheryl M. Sigmon • Scholastic Teaching Resources • Lesson 25

breathe	valentine
committee	shrapnel
desert	vandal
discussed	diesel
either	Braille
mesmerize	maverick

a e e i l n n s t v

embarrassed	cereal
enough	hygiene
especially	mentor
everywhere	panacea
excellent	volcano
atlas	electricity

a a b e e m m n r r s s t

Systematic Word Study for Grades 4–6 © 2011 by Cheryl M. Sigmon • Scholastic Teaching Resources • Lesson 27

foreign	ambience
frighten	bizarre
height	brochure
himself	entourage
humorous	impromptu
cliché	debris

a   a   l   m   o   o   p   p   r   s

hungry	chocolate
immediately	hurricane
its	tornado
knowledge	canyon
square	canoe
cafeteria	avocado

a c e h i n r r s u

 Systematic Word Study for Grades 4–6 © 2011 by Cheryl M. Sigmon • Scholastic Teaching Resources • Lesson 29

necessary	magazine
neighbor	colonel
ourselves	incognito
once	alfresco
people	hamburger
alcohol	schema

a c e h i k o r s t

receive	distinct
recommend	rugged
separate	glamorous
themselves	grotesque
usually	unsightly
elegant	shadowy

a c d e e i n o r s t

Systematic Word Study for Grades 4–6 © 2011 by Cheryl M. Sigmon • Scholastic Teaching Resources • Lesson 31

though	diminutive
thought	colossal
through	enormous
throughout	microscopic
you're	voluminous
your	immense

a e i i m n r t u

weight	employer
where	permanent
seriously	temporary
quiet	chronological
oxymoron	dependents
applicant	references

b e e e f f g i i n n r t s

Systematic Word Study for Grades 4–6 © 2011 by Cheryl M. Sigmon • Scholastic Teaching Resources • Lesson 33

familiar	decade
favorite	intermittent
experience	annual
tendency	periodic
ancient	sporadic
continual	lengthy

a e f n n o o r s t

because	brazenly
divergent	casually
Europe	cautiously
ocean	cowardly
adamantly	cynically
anxiously	eerily

e i i l n n s s t t y

Systematic Word Study for Grades 4–6 © 2011 by Cheryl M. Sigmon • Scholastic Teaching Resources • Lesson 35

Linkage Word Strips

Week 1: snaproblemergenericompletedearefercertaindexamplentypequestionsubookrecaptionlyearebibliographyarnits

Week 2: bunheardentrancentobtusesincenteroofriendsoapiecellusuallyardacutemperorganizebraccuracyclonecomputationational

Week 3: herbivoredcatchappeneducatenemysteriousubecomemorialhadaptationomnivoregulatecamouflagenderacrosshoweverycarnivore

Week 4: hamendmentemperememberreachedgearlyriconstitutioncellistenvelopedallowholedocumentpreambledgejuryellowheelevator

Week 5: lesseveralwaysimilengthhimselfableopardentvowelegenrecoveryieldimorningermetaphorganizebramysteryespeciallyical

Week 6: butruexamplessonumeralapatternestagainsteadiameteradiusecretionaprobabilityranticompositehundreduceequadranthrifty

Week 7: soldierslowlyescapecologyroscopecosystemusclearmadillovoicesubiomenoticementabiospherecriediscussouthermos

Week 8: symphonylongroundillovablegislativexecutivertextravelevatorderrandisastercertaintroducenteroofigurejudicialoconjunctions

Week 9: Englishadowaitselfinallyricorrectaxinterjectionlineutralliterationboardeeproofreadocanalogymanightmarequireqotations

Week 10: adverbalancexponentrancentralashownicknamendeeparallelogramasstreetvertextendinchestatentinchesquicklyearconvextra

Week 11: reachemicaloreproducellardec:deditordinalapotentialackineticrazyachthermalicecoursecuresurfacetiousamechanicalculate

Week 12: begannextrememoirevenueboycottacobjectarparagraphaseasyetagovernmenteramongoneimmigrantibioticannoticensus

Week 13: didiomachineutraleaplanetworknotsystemicroscopeasuperlativertexiticlauselfunderstandabroughtechyperboleanquarantine

Week 14: beginequalitypequilateraliendigitshelfairatioilanguagequationlinexplainothoughosthousandsavortexvolumeterminatempt

Week 22: intercommunismallambesideediscoveredevelopedestriangleafinishedimperialismuglyesocialismilliontoperhapsofascism

Week 23: weathermaliciousnakestrangerspiderstruggleeggiraffebbloodrivingloathunderodecimalicensoribridgestureadarknessentialthird

Week 24: disheartenedeucateacheriditypethnologyearepresentencertainewhethereeflowerskeletonclothesitateamindermatologymnistamen

Week 25: insecticidescribebehavioringerlyricaloriefincisionanothermoscissorsalthougherbicideglobeliefibeneathumpapersonification

Week 26: navalentineitherrandesertandememesmerizenithesishrapneleadiscussedimenteamavericknotubreatheediselectelecommitteeth

Week 28: lambiancentereforeignorthumorousefuleafrightentouragenuisaidebrislandetacheightengagebizarrepairbrochurentimpromptu

Week 30: pourselvesselhalfresconcentricolonelephantincognitopeoplethalcoholyeareignecessaryearneighborschemagazinerthamburger

Week 32: beneathoughosthroughoutensioncenormousayournimblediminutivecolossaluteethoughtimmenservevoluminousemicroscopic

Week 34: pretendencyderannualeafavoritexperiencedecadeafamiliartfulengthyroidealintermittentancientertainaperiodicontinualsporadic

Word Clusters

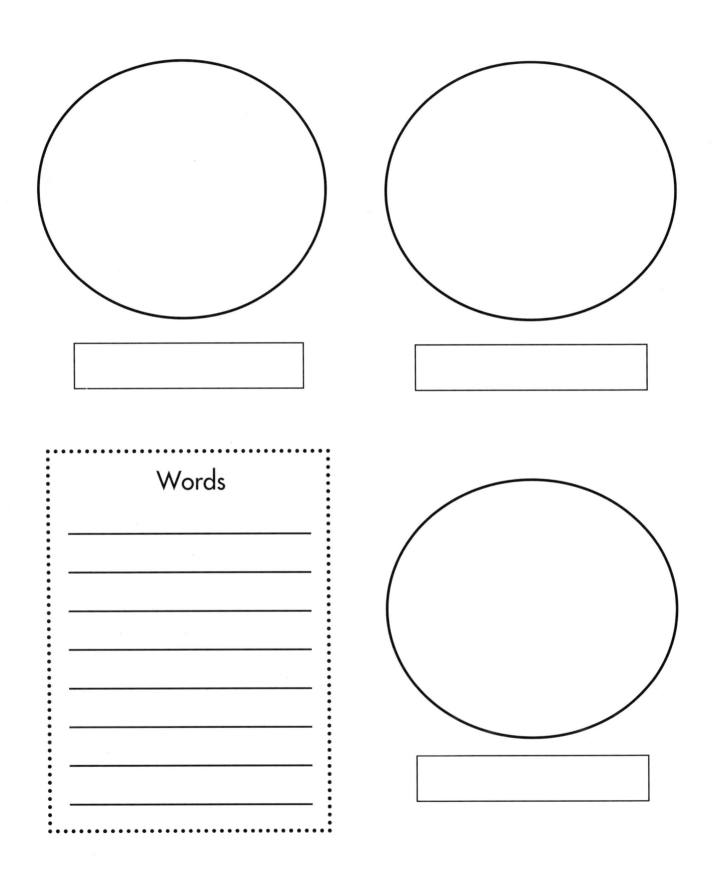

Words

Systematic Word Study for Grades 4–6 © 2011 by Cheryl M. Sigmon • Scholastic Teaching Resources